W9-BMB-840

awake my soul

awake my soul

Contemporary Catholics on Traditional Devotions

edited by James Martin, S.J.

LOYOLAPRESS.

CHICAGO

LOYOLAPRESS.

3441 N. ASHLAND AVENUE
CHICAGO, ILLINOIS 60657
(800) 621-1008
WWW.LOYOLABOOKS.ORG

© 2004 James Martin, S.J.
All rights reserved

Imprimi Potest: Very Rev. Thomas J. Regan, S.J.

Cover photo: © Mel Curtis/Getty Images
Cover and interior design by Megan Duffy Rostan

Library of Congress Cataloging-in-Publication Data
Awake my soul : contemporary Catholics on traditional
devotions / edited by James Martin.

     p. cm.
Includes bibliographical references.
   ISBN 0-8294-1987-X
  1.   Spiritual life—Catholic Church. 2.   Devotional
literature. 3.   Catholic Church—Prayer-books and devotions. I.   Martin, James, S.J.
   BX2178.A93 2004
   248.4'6'088282—dc22

                        2003109401

Printed in the United States of America.
03 04 05 06 07 08 Versa 10 9 8 7 6 5 4 3 2 1

This book is dedicated to my
spiritual directors, past and present,
who have, in countless ways,
helped me to find God in all things.

My heart is steadfast, O God, my heart is steadfast;
  I will sing and make melody.
  Awake, my soul!
Awake, O harp and lyre!
  I will awake the dawn.

Ps 108:1–2

contents

Contents

Introduction

A surprising number of recent books and studies have suggested that young American Catholics are more likely than their immediate elders to gravitate toward traditional devotions. The reasons seem varied. Some surmise that younger Catholics, having grown up without being "forced" to participate in devotions, have no built-in reactions against them. Freer to embrace or ignore devotions, many choose to embrace them. Others see in this phenomenon a turn toward conservatism among younger Catholics. Still others posit that the characteristics of the devotional life—tactile, colorful, often exotic—exert a particular influence on young Catholics seeking a greater sense of mystery in their lives.

For some older Catholics, the devotional life has never lost its appeal. Many fondly remember reciting the Rosary with parents, attending novena services (and singing special novena hymns) at their home parish, or receiving their first Miraculous Medal or scapular from a favorite aunt or uncle. Devotions can represent a powerful affective link to the Catholicism of one's youth while continuing to nourish one's faith as an adult.

But for other Catholics the topic of devotions can provoke decidedly uncomfortable reactions. Though expressions of popular piety have long been a part of Catholicism, some see devotions as inconsistent with a mature faith, antithetical to a contemporary understanding of religion, overly reliant on *things*—beads, medals, scapulars—and even faintly superstitious. For some, devotions are to be avoided, not embraced.

This wide variety of reactions raises some important questions: What do traditional devotions have to say to contemporary Catholics? How might a devotion that has seen its popularity wax and wane (and now wax again) speak to Catholics unfamiliar with its appeal? Can devotions that sometimes carry heavy theological and cultural "baggage" find a place in the post–Vatican II church? In short, what might devotions mean today?

To begin to explore these questions, I asked a number of Catholics, some in their thirties and forties, to address this issue in a series originally published, in a much abbreviated form, in *America* magazine. Each contributor was asked to write about a devotion that has proved especially meaningful in his or her life as a Catholic. Each was also asked to provide a brief historical sketch and to discuss what the devotion might mean to other Catholics in current times.

As many of our essayists note, the theological question of the role of devotions in today's church is a complex one. For while devotions have historically played an important role in Catholic spirituality, they need always be seen as flowing from (and leading back to) the liturgy—the central form of worship in the church. The Second Vatican Council wrote that while devotions should be "warmly commended" and possess a "special dignity," they nevertheless remain subordinate to the Mass, which "by its very nature far surpasses any of them."[1] Theologians and liturgical scholars have therefore rightly cautioned against devotions usurping the place of the liturgy in the life of the faithful.

Indeed, in the past, excesses in popular piety may have led some Catholics to focus their spiritual lives on a particular devotion rather than on participation in the Eucharist—for example, if the celebration of the Mass at their local parish was not to their liking. ("Why should I go to Mass? I have my Rosary.") Today, however, the tendency may be the opposite: to dismiss devotions as if they had no meaning or relevance whatsoever.

Both reactions go against the grain of our Catholic heritage. A comprehensive guide published by the Vatican in 2001 noted that "the Liturgy and popular piety are two forms of worship which are in mutual and fruitful relationship with each other."[2] In other words, there is no conflict between loving the Mass and, say, having a devotion to the Sacred Heart of

Jesus. The document expressed the hope that "other forms of piety among the Christian people are not overlooked, nor their useful contribution to living in unity with Christ, in the Church, be forgotten."[3]

This little book tries to highlight that "useful contribution." In the next few pages our essayists offer their reflections on the Sacred Heart of Jesus, adoration of the Blessed Sacrament, pilgrimages, the saints, the Angelus, litanies, the Miraculous Medal, novenas, the Rosary, holy water, Our Lady of Guadalupe, First Fridays, *lectio divina,* the Immaculate Heart, relics, the Liturgy of the Hours, Mary, Joseph, and the stations of the cross.

Obviously, this loose list of devotions is not meant to be exhaustive. In fact, the very concept of "devotions" often seems difficult to define adequately or even describe with precision. *The Encyclopedia of Catholicism,* for example, defines *devotions* as follows: "Nonliturgical prayer forms that promote affective (and sometimes individualistic) attitudes of faith. They may also suggest a more effective response to personal religious needs than liturgical prayer."[4] *The*

New Dictionary of Theology begins its lengthy and comprehensive entry with a brief statement: "Devotions are the feeling side of Christian faith."[5]

But for those unfamiliar with devotions such definitions, while certainly accurate, may raise as many questions as they answer. The first definition implies that *any* religious practice outside the liturgy is a devotion. The second suggests that while the devotional life evokes "feelings," the liturgical life does not. Complicating matters somewhat, the Vatican document defines devotions as "various external practices (e.g., prayers, hymns, observances attached to particular times or places, insignia, medals, habits or customs)" but at the same time distinguishes them from "pious exercises," "popular piety," and "popular religiosity."[6]

The difficulty in providing a concise definition of devotions reflects the fact that the devotional life encompasses an astonishingly wide variety of practices and traditions. As a result, it's often difficult to agree on what, precisely, constitutes a devotion. When some of these essays originally ran in *America,* for example, a few readers wrote to ask why I had included the Liturgy of the Hours, which they felt was more properly considered a "liturgy," not a devotion. Here one can see how the boundaries and definitions remain sketchy: the Liturgy of the Hours is indeed a liturgy, especially when celebrated in a communal setting; but when practiced individually, as described by our essayist, it takes on more the quality and flavor of a traditional private devotion.

Needless to say, then, this collection is not meant to include every devotion in the Catholic tradition. (It is, in fact, doubtful that such a list could even be agreed upon!) Rather, it tries to encompass some devotions that may be ripe for a kind of renewal, or that have fallen into desuetude, or that may be less well known or understood by contemporary Catholics. Each of these traditional devotions, however, continues to exert a powerful and undeniable influence on our writers and, not incidentally, on a great many of the People of God.

The riches of the devotional life speak to millions of Catholics whose faith was nurtured in a world where devotions played an important role in their religious education. Today, these same devotions speak in a particular way to younger Catholics eager to rediscover their Catholic heritage, to explore new ways of prayer, and to regain a sense of mystery in their lives. As these essays reveal, the devotional life can move us to prayer and contemplation, comfort us in times of suffering or confusion, encourage us to care for others, spur us on to appreciate Scripture more fully, provide us with models of Christian discipleship, prompt us to meditate on the love of God, and, overall, draw us closer to the One who lies at the center of any expression of our faith: Jesus Christ.

The Sacred Heart
of Jesus

CHRISTOPHER J. RUDDY, thirty-two, is an assistant professor of theology at the University of St. Thomas in St. Paul, Minnesota. After graduating from Yale University in 1993, he worked with the Jesuit Volunteer Corps before entering Harvard Divinity School, where he completed a master's degree in theological studies. In 2001 he received a Ph.D. in systematic theology from the University of Notre Dame. Today Mr. Ruddy and his wife, Deborah Wallace, live with their one-year-old son, Peter Augustine, in St. Paul.

....

Seventy-two times a minute, 4,320 times an hour, 103,680 times a day, almost 38 million times a year—over 2.6 billion times in the course of an average life. Fist sized, the human heart beats powerfully and durably. It must be sturdy enough to contract and send fresh blood throughout the entire body, elastic enough to collect spent, deoxygenated blood. Too much hardness or softness of heart, and one dies. Only a healthy heart—strong and supple—can give and receive lifeblood.

Devotion to the Sacred Heart of Jesus has suffered cardiac arrest in recent decades. It has been dismissed as superstitious in its apparent guarantee of salvation to those who practice it, as masochistic in its emphasis on making reparation for Jesus' own suffering. Its popular iconography is—to put it generously—saccharine, kitschy, effeminate, somehow ethereal and grotesque at once. This decline of devotion is all the more striking because of its preeminence in the first half of the twentieth century, when so many Catholic families had a picture of Jesus and his Sacred Heart displayed in their homes, and when Thursday-night holy hours and First Fridays proliferated in parishes.

Like many forms of heart disease, such atrophy could have been prevented through a healthy diet—in this case, Scripture and tradition. The heart is a powerful metaphor in the Bible, what Karl Rahner, S.J., has called a "primordial word." It signifies the wellspring of life, the totality of one's being. The prophet Ezekiel, for instance, records God's promise to change Israel's "heart of stone" into a "heart of flesh," while John's Gospel gives the heart its most profound scriptural expression: Jesus' heart is the source of living water, of rest for the Beloved Disciple, of the church and its sacraments, of doubting Thomas's faith.

Devotion to the Sacred Heart began to flourish in the Middle Ages through a renewed attentiveness to Jesus' humanity and his Passion. Its golden age, though, was the seventeenth century, when Francis de Sales, Jane de Chantal, and what was called the "French School" offered a tender, compassionate spirituality that helped to renew the church and counter Jansenism's severity and sectarianism. From 1673 to 1675 at the Visitation convent of Paray-le-Monial, Margaret Mary Alacoque received a series of four revelations from Christ about his heart. It was here that the devotion reached its enduring form: personal consecration to the Sacred Heart, the observance of an hour of prayer on Thursday night between eleven o'clock and midnight as a way of sharing in Christ's suffering in Gethsemane, and the reception of communion on the first Friday of the month as reparation for the indignities inflicted upon the sacrament by those indifferent and ungrateful. This last revelation would evolve into a belief that salvation was assured to those who received communion on the first Fridays of nine consecutive months.

The Sacred Heart was later enlisted in combat against the French Revolution, Communism, and threats to family life. Pope Pius IX made it a feast of the universal church in 1856, and Leo XIII consecrated the entire world to the Sacred Heart in 1899. The devotion reached its magisterial peak in Pius XII's 1956 encyclical *Haurietis Aquas* ("You Shall Draw Waters"), which emphasized God's passionate love for humanity.

I believe that the deepest meaning of the devotion, however, is glimpsed in a poet who does not even mention it: Dante Alighieri. At the dark bottom of hell, Satan is frozen in ice up to his chest, crying tears and drooling bloody foam, his six wings bellowing cold wind upward. Wedged into the inverted apex of the underworld, he is locked in his own resentment, impotent and utterly alone. Hell, the *Inferno* makes clear, is not fire, but ice: cold, crabbed isolation. Paradise is pure communion, illuminated and warmed by the love that moves the sun and the other stars.

I did not grow up with any devotion to the Sacred Heart, and it is only in the last few years, as I have struggled with vocation and the demands of family life, that the practice has spoken to my own heart: the fearful heart that paralyzes me when I think of the future, rendering me unable to open myself in trust to God; the cramped heart that refuses to admit my wife and infant son but clings to my own prerogatives, choosing to watch Peter out of the corner of my eye as I read the morning newspaper rather than get on the floor and play with him; the oblivious heart that holds forth at dinner on the recording history of the Beatles' *Abbey Road* but forgets to ask Deborah how her class went that afternoon. At times like these I wonder, *Have I really let into my life those I love so much? Have I gone out to them? Are they part of my flesh or merely fellow travelers?*

On a particularly difficult afternoon last summer, I took Peter for a walk. We wound up at a church in our neighborhood, and, almost unable to bear the despair and self-loathing that were consuming me, I went in to pray. I lit a candle before Mary for my wife and one for myself before Joseph. Almost accidentally, I stopped in front of a woodcarving of the Sacred Heart. Caught somewhere between rage and tears, I looked up at the heart and, for the first time, saw beyond the barbed-wire crown of thorns encircling it, into its gentleness. A prayer rose up in me: *Jesus, give me a bigger heart.* I looked at Peter in shame and in hope, and I went out into the day.

I remain irritable and irritating. I continue to struggle with a stoniness that shuts out so many. I know ever more clearly my deep sinfulness. But in continuing to pray to the Sacred Heart, I have also come to know God's still deeper mercy. I am strengthened by a heart pierced but unvanquished. I am welcomed by a heart that knows only tenderness and so makes me tender. I look on that pulsing, fleshy heart: courageous and vulnerable, compact and capacious, never one without the other.

The Angelus

EMILIE GRIFFIN is the author of a number of books on the spiritual life, including *Turning: Reflections on the Experience of Conversion, Clinging: The Experience of Prayer,* and the recent *Doors into Prayer,* which has also been published in Britain. Ms. Griffin is active in Renovaré, an organization dedicated to Christian renewal with an ecumenical focus. She and her husband, William, live in Alexandria, Louisiana, and are the parents of three adult children. They have two grandchildren.

....

M y first memory of hearing the Angelus prayed was on a hillside in Mexico. We were in a country place not far from Puebla. American college students were wandering around to get a sense of the culture and to see the sights. I was not a Catholic then and was only gradually learning how religion had been suppressed in Mexico.

But there, suddenly, was a picture on a hillside, almost like something from the Renaissance: the church, the bell tower, the people in a nearby field falling to their knees. One of them was a sister in full habit, a rare sight in Mexico then.

Our guide was a U.S. graduate student who knew Mexico well. "They're saying the Angelus," he explained.

Well, I thought I knew something about the Catholic faith, because I had been raised in New Orleans. But—saying the Angelus? To me, it was brand new.

The Angelus is an ancient prayer in honor of the Incarnation. It is repeated three times a day—ideally at the sound of a bell. There are four versicles, three Hail Marys, and a concluding prayer. Originally the Angelus was properly said kneeling, except on Saturdays and Sundays, when a standing posture was required. But in the twentieth century the rules were relaxed somewhat. Still, the prayers need to be said at more or less the proper times: morning, noon, and evening. The praying thus becomes part of the rhythm of the day.

The whole Angelus as commonly printed should be recited. But if you don't have the text, don't know the prayers by heart, or if you can't read, you can say five Hail Marys instead.

And yes, there's an indulgence given to those who say the Angelus. An indulgence of one hundred days for each recitation, with a plenary indulgence once a month, was attached to the prayer by Pope Benedict XIII on September 14, 1724. The conditions for reciting the prayer and receiving the indulgence were somewhat relaxed by Leo XIII on April 3, 1884.

But the sweetness of this devotion, I think, has more to do with the declaring than the receiving:

The Angel of the Lord declared unto Mary.
Angelus Domini nuntiavit Mariae.

Some great essentials of Catholic faith are captured in this prayer.

Here is the whole devotion as it is commonly said today:

VERSE: The Angel of the Lord declared unto Mary,
RESPONSE: *And she conceived of the Holy Spirit.*

Hail Mary, full of grace, the Lord is with thee . . .
VERSE: Behold the handmaid of the Lord.
RESPONSE: *Be it done unto me according to your word.*

Hail Mary, full of grace, the Lord is with thee . . .
VERSE: And the Word was made flesh,
RESPONSE: *And dwelt among us.*

Hail Mary, full of grace, the Lord is with thee . . .
VERSE: Pray for us, O Holy Mother of God,
RESPONSE: *That we may be worthy of the promises of Christ.*

Let us pray:
Pour forth, we beseech you, O Lord, your grace into our hearts; that, as we have known the incarnation of Christ, your son, by the message of an angel, so by his

passion and cross we may be brought to the glory of his
resurrection. Through the same Christ, our Lord. Amen.

In Scripture the angel who declared unto Mary
was the archangel Gabriel. The angelic name,
Gabriel, has proved a clue for scholars who want to
trace the history of the Angelus. In an attempt to
document the ringing of the Angelus in England and
Europe in the thirteenth and fourteenth centuries,
studies were made of inscriptions on church bells
surviving from that era. In England especially, a large
number of church bells of that period bear Gabriel's
name. The bells have charming inscriptions: *Dulcis
instar mellis campana vocor Gabrielis* ("I am sweet as
honey, and I am called Gabriel's bell"); *Ecce Gabrielis
sonat haec campana fidelis* ("Behold the bell of faithful Gabriel sounds"); *Missi de coelis nomen habeo
Gabrielis* ("I bear the name of Gabriel sent from
heaven"); *Missus vero pie Gabriel fert laeta Mariae*
("Gabriel the messenger brings joyous tidings to holy
Mary"); and many more. The scholars concluded

that these must have been Angelus bells, for though the archangel Michael was far and away the more popular patron in England, many more bells are inscribed for Gabriel.

It seems that the practice of ringing and reciting the Angelus grew out of an earlier practice of saying three Hail Marys at sunset, which became general throughout Europe in the first half of the fourteenth century. This prayer was indulgenced and recommended by Pope John XXII in 1318 and 1327. The recitation of Hail Marys at the Compline bell was recorded much earlier than this in Europe and the British Isles, apparently tied to a belief that this was the very hour when the angel spoke to Mary. Some historians trace the Angelus to prayers said at the tolling of the curfew bell, first recorded in Normandy in 1061. The full Angelus, corresponding to our modern prayer, is first found in printed form in 1612. Variations occur in different locales; in Italy a De Profundis was recited for the holy souls immediately after the evening Angelus. Another variation, also Italian, adds three Glorias to the Angelus in thanksgiving for Mary's privileges.

Only last year a parish church near us in Alexandria, Louisiana, installed a new bell tower. And yes, among the many peals it plays in its electronic circuit, the Angelus sounds three times daily as it did in former times and places far away.

One recent book, *Prayers for Midday* (Liturgy Training Publications, 1999), a small collection of timeless prayers, recommends praying the Angelus with non-Catholics and presents a formula for doing so.

However we pray it, whenever we do, the wonder of the Incarnation becomes present to us as it did to our ancestors in faith.

Once, when I was making a weeklong retreat high in the Colorado mountains, at Nada Hermitage in Crestone, the Angelus bell happened to sound just when I was making a long-distance call. After I had placed the call, the Angelus bell began to ring.

When my husband answered, I said, "Oh, my timing is off—they're ringing the Angelus."

"No, your timing is perfect," he responded.
And we said the Angelus together:

The Angel of the Lord declared unto Mary,
And she conceived of the Holy Spirit.
Hail Mary, full of grace, the Lord is with thee. . . .

What century is it? I found myself thinking. But then I decided the Incarnation belongs to all places and times.

First Fridays

RON HANSEN is the author of several novels, including *Mariette in Ecstasy, Hitler's Niece,* and *Atticus,* which was a National Book Award finalist. His most recent novel is *Isn't It Romantic?* Mr. Hansen is also the author of *A Stay against Confusion: Essays on Faith and Fiction* and the short-story collection *Nebraska.* He is the Gerard Manley Hopkins, S.J., Professor of Arts and Humanities at Santa Clara University and lives with his wife, the writer Bo Caldwell, in Cupertino, California.

....

A few years ago the late Lou Bannan, S.J., was presiding at the noontime Mass on a first Friday of the month at Santa Clara University. In his homily he told us about ferrying a group of older retreatants to the San Jose airport and hearing them rave about a fellow Jesuit who'd wowed them with his wisdom, caring, and holiness. There was no temperance to their praise. Lou just hunched over the steering wheel and kept driving until one of the retreatants noticed his silence and confided, "We're sure you're very holy, too, Fr. Bannan."

Lou smiled and wryly answered, "Oh, you don't have to worry about *me*. I've made the nine First Fridays."

He was referring to a practice initiated by St. Margaret Mary Alacoque, a Sister of the Visitation in Paray-le-Monial, France. She reported to her Jesuit confessor, St. Claude La Colombière, that in a series of apparitions that commenced in December 1673, Jesus had revealed to her his infinite love for humanity and his hurt over so much coldness and ingratitude to him. She said Christ sought to encourage devotion to his Sacred Heart through a number of promises (generally counted as twelve), the final one being this: "In the excess of the mercy of my heart, I promise you that my all-powerful love will grant to all those who shall receive Communion on the first Friday of nine consecutive months the grace of final repentance: they shall not die in my displeasure nor without receiving the sacraments; and my heart will be their safe refuge in that last hour."

Conditions were added, probably by church authorities. Confession was required within eight days. Communicants were to have the proper disposition, that is, awareness and reverence. And they were to receive the Eucharist with the conscious intention of making reparation to the Sacred Heart of Jesus and in order to warrant the graces of Christ's promises.

A skewed view of the devotion might imply that it skirts rather closely to Pelagianism—the fifth-century heresy that supposes we can effect our own salvation. But in fact Jesus, not our exertions, is primary in the devotion, and the only guarantee is that we will be predisposed to Christian discipleship through frequent reception of the sacraments.

Skeptics might also argue that Christ's revelations seem whiny and more like the overwrought imaginings of a peasant nun who was famously unhappy in her convent. She may have invented the conversations just to seem special. But few of Christ's locutions to mystics over the centuries have actually sounded like the Jesus of the Gospels—he uses their language, not his own—and Fr. La Colombière was convinced of Sister Margaret Mary's veracity, as was Pope Benedict XV, who canonized her.

When I was in my Catholic grade school and high school, it was a given that there would be a First Friday Mass so the students could fulfill Christ's conditions and find assurance in his promises; and even now, three hundred years after the saint's death, the practice she introduced is still so widely accepted that parishes generally plan for greater Mass attendance on the first Friday of the month.

There seem to be three reasons why. The first, of course, is that it all could be true: that no matter what befalls us, Christ will be available to us in our final hours.

But the second reason seems just as interesting: that Catholics are a Lenten people who recognize the value of piety and strict disciplines. Economists and sociologists have puzzled over a paradox: the religion that seems easiest and exacts the least from its congregations would seem to be most attractive, but the opposite is true, no matter the culture or geography. Those religions that seem superficially hardest are the ones that are gaining in membership, while those that are most lax are declining in numbers.

And the third reason for the continued popularity of the nine First Fridays is that they present such a vital metaphor for what the Christian project is all about, uniting as they do the Lenten and Good Friday image of Christ's atoning sacrifice for our sins, and the nine-month, Advent image of pregnancy and expectation. In our Eucharist, our thanksgiving, we worship God made flesh, we remember and celebrate our redemption on the cross, and we look forward to the peaceable kingdom that is still in the process of being born.

The Immaculate
Heart of Mary

JANICE FARNHAM, R.J.M., is a member of the Religious of Jesus and Mary and a professor of church history at Weston Jesuit School of Theology in Cambridge, Massachusetts. There she teaches, among other courses, "The History of Christian Spirituality" and "Popular Religion since the French Revolution." Sister Janice has taught at Trinity College in Hartford, Connecticut, and at the Washington Theological Union. She also has worked in the South Bronx as an advocate for children in public schools and has served as a member of the leadership team of her province.

....

In the cold December half-light where I sat with my first cup of coffee, it caught my eye. I was intent on praying myself into a good attitude for a weekend of meetings and saw outside my window one of many astounding ironies in midtown Manhattan. There, in the middle of a tiny convent garden, stood a slender statue of the Sacred Heart. The familiar Jesus of my childhood pointed to his heart and blessed the oblivious multitudes rushing down East Thirty-third Street. It was a comforting and nostalgic sight. I recited some lines from a favorite hymn: "Heart of my own heart, whatever befall . . . Still be my vision."

But wait a minute. What was that on his head?

It was a veil. My "vision" needed some tweaking.

The view was not of Jesus, but of Mary. It was not his heart, but hers, transfixed by the sword of the world's pain and sorrows, as Simeon predicted, "that the thoughts of many hearts may be revealed" (Lk 2:35). To Jesus through Mary, I remembered. For Jesus, through her heart to ours.

Generations have found comfort in Mary's heart as a shining mirror of Christ's own, a tangible symbol of the compassion and mercy of God in womanly guise. Like other forms of Marian piety, devotion to Mary's heart has undergone numerous historical variations. At different times, pious folk have been drawn to Mary's "Holy," "Sacred," "Most Pure," and, more familiarly, "Immaculate" heart.

Rooted in the scriptural texts of Luke's infancy narratives, Christian attention to the heart of Mary provides a central theme for discipleship: "Mary kept all these things, pondering them in her heart" (Lk 2:19). In fact, the biblical "heart" (in Greek, *kardia*) is a word far richer than its popular association with love and human affectivity. It embraces the deeper elements of courage, insight, knowledge, deep desire, and will. Throughout the Gospel the figure of Mary, as the first disciple, contemplates and treasures the mystery to which she has freely surrendered herself without fully understanding it. In Ignatian terms, Mary's heart is the center of her experiential, *felt* knowledge of God in Christ, her son and savior. It describes her personality, that passionate and patient love for the one she knows "by heart," as well as her constancy and faithful seeking, without seeing, along what mystics name the "way of unknowing." Mary is called to bear the drama and tragedy of her own people, as she bears God's Word in her body and in her heart. In this she becomes the prototype of the new Israel, as prophesied by Jeremiah and Ezekiel, with God's law written on her heart, a heart of flesh and not of stone.

Patristic and medieval writings picked up on these biblical images, referring to Mary's heart as the source of her *fiat*. He shed the blood of his body; she, the blood of her heart. St. Augustine reminded his community that Mary was more blessed for having borne Christ in her heart than in her flesh. The first known prayer invoking the heart of Mary, composed in 1184 by Ekbert of Schonau, calls on all to "praise the happiness of your heart, whence our salvation flowed." At the Cistercian monastery of Helfta, a center of women's spirituality in the thirteenth century, interest in the devotion was promoted by its renowned visionaries, Mechtild of Hackeborn and Gertrude the Great. Medieval Franciscan theologians, especially Bernardine of Siena, wrote of Mary's heart as a "furnace of divine love," stressing the affective dimensions of the symbol.

The devotion deepened in seventeenth-century Europe, thanks to the insights of a generation of apostles, founders, and mystics, all leaders of what came to be known as the "French School." A major emphasis of this spirituality was the Incarnate Word, revealed in the mysteries of self-emptying and love as symbolized in Christ's infancy, passion, and death. Mary was the perfect mirror of that Word, her heart echoing the sentiments of Christ's own. From this time on, the two "sacred hearts" of Jesus and Mary would lay claim to Catholic piety for imitation, but even more, for veneration and reparation. Filling an affective vacuum created by rationalism, this approach met with great success at the level of popular piety. It also ignited violent Jansenist opposition and theological squabbles with Jesuits and others who were accused of promoting an all-too-earthy "new devotion."

The most notable advance in devotion to the heart of Mary can be attributed to St. John Eudes, who composed texts for a proper Mass and office, which he hoped would be adopted by the universal church. He also founded several religious societies dedicated to promoting the devotion. Just before his death in 1681, Eudes finished a major treatise, *The Admirable Heart of Mary*. His dream of an approved cult and feast, however, would not be realized until 1855, when the Congregation of Rites approved private celebrations of the "Most Pure Heart of Mary." And only in 1944 did Pope Pius XII extend the liturgical celebration to the universal church, assigning the feast to August 22, the octave of the Assumption. With the liturgical reforms of the Second Vatican Council, the memorial of the Immaculate Heart of Mary was transferred to a more fitting date: the Saturday following the Feast of the Sacred Heart.

Many Catholics of a certain age will easily recall the importance given to the Immaculate Heart in the wake of the appearances of Our Lady of Fatima in Portugal during 1917. There Mary had reportedly given the three child visionaries a mission "to establish world devotion to my Immaculate Heart." Her message of prayer, penance, and reparation—coming as it did in the wake of Soviet Communism—brought Mary's heart into the global conflicts of the twentieth century and into the consciousness of millions of young Catholics.

In the last cantos of his *Paradiso,* Dante addresses Mary as *figlia del tuo Figlio*—"daughter of your Son"—and describes her face as the one that most resembles Christ's. Such poetic images reveal the grace of a unique bond between Jesus and Mary, a sacred mutuality of likeness. It is rooted in the exquisite, profoundly physical relationship of mother and son.

As I write these lines, my niece Erin is about to give birth to her first child. She has explained to me that her heart pumps blood into the placenta that nourishes the baby in her womb. In a very real sense, Erin's heart has become—like every mother's—her child's lifeline. So it was, I like to think, between Mary and Jesus. Her heart's blood flowed into his tiny frame, feeding his body from her own, announcing the Eucharist. Her heart's *yes* to God's mystery mothered him for mission in those long years at Nazareth we now call the "hidden life." She and Joseph taught him how to treasure that mystery in the Scriptures, in nature, and in the events of his life. She must have encouraged Jesus to seek and follow his unique call, even if sometimes she and others he loved might not have understood what he did or said. Like all parents, Mary learned to let her child go and grow in freedom, all the way to Calvary, even if it broke her heart many times over.

I have to admit that until now I haven't really paid much attention to Mary's heart in my own personal prayer. Maybe that's what God wanted me to learn through this little reflection. Noticed or forgotten, desired or resisted, bidden or unbidden, Mary's heart is *there,* for all of us, and for all the ignored, unloved, unloving, wayward children she has mothered in Christ. What it was for Jesus, it is for me: a pledge and a presence of the love that never fails, "whatever befall." As the reality of global violence threatens the future of our world, the pierced heart of Mary, home of the Spirit, can still be my vision, one I trust and treasure, even in the cold half-light of these ominous times.

The Stations
of the Cross

THERESE J. BORCHARD, thirty-one, writes the syndi-
cated column "Our Turn," distributed by Catholic News
Service. She is the coeditor, with Michael Leach, of the best-
selling *I Like Being Catholic: Treasured Traditions, Rituals,
and Stories* and *I Like Being Married,* and is the author of
*Winging It: Meditations of a Young Adult, Our Catholic
Devotions: A Popular Guidebook,* as well as several other
books. She holds a master's degree in theology from the
University of Notre Dame and lives with her husband, Eric,
and son, David, in Annapolis, Maryland.

....

January 12, 1995, is etched permanently in
my memory. My father, suffering a fatal bout
of bronchial pneumonia, died peacefully at

approximately eight o'clock in the evening, in the intensive care unit of Kettering Memorial Hospital in Dayton, Ohio.

I will forever remember the details leading up to and following that sacred moment, when I held his hand in mine and witnessed firsthand his spirit escape his body, leaving the cold shell of a corpse behind.

Every January 12, I commemorate the date by calling my sisters and sharing favorite memories of my dad, by pulling out some old photos, by stealing a few still minutes in the day's disorder and allowing myself some tears. I take time to remember because I never want to forget.

The stations of the cross serve the same purpose: to remember Jesus.

According to legend, Mary was the first to walk the Way of Sorrows. As any grieving mother would, she returned to the last places she saw her son, and remembered him. Stopping along the way—where he began carrying the cross, where he fell, where the nails penetrated his flesh, and where he ultimately died—she poured out her grief and reflected on the awesome miracle of his life. The earliest Christians followed her example. By walking the dirt road to Calvary, by witnessing the holiest of places, they could better remember the sacrifice he endured for them.

As the desire to walk the Way of Calvary intensified in the succeeding centuries, so did the need to replicate the experience, an alternative pilgrimage, so to speak, for those who couldn't make the arduous journey. Even those who had visited the shrines in Jerusalem wanted representations of them closer to home so they could remember and honor the passion of the Lord in some way. Imitations of the more important shrines in Jerusalem began to spring up in various places, for example, at the Monastery of San Stefano in Bologna.

By the fourteenth century, copies of the Church of the Holy Sepulchre and other shrines, known as "Little Jerusalems," could be found all over Europe. And by the fifteenth century, carvings and pictorial representations of the holy places in Jerusalem were arranged in many small churches and large religious institutions throughout Europe, providing the faithful everywhere access to the devotion. In 1731 the number (fourteen) and the sequence of stations were set by Pope Clement XII, though these were determined more by devotional writers in Europe than by the practice of pilgrims in the Holy Land.

No matter how big, small, elaborate, or simple the carvings or pictorial representations that today hang on church walls in virtually every country of the world, they direct our minds and souls to Jesus, fourteen stopping points along the way to his death; they are snapshots of the man who died to save us from ourselves, a kind of storybook on the wall describing the Christian journey to redemption.

For me, the stations are the heart of Lent. Each year, at the most depressing time of year, when the days are shortest, coldest, and darkest, I amble into church to celebrate the story that places my worries and tribulations into proper context.

I smell the incense and remember how Jenny Sand would faint every Friday afternoon in between sung stanzas of "Were You There?" and "Ashes" as our sixth-grade class gathered for the stations. I listen to the narrator describe how Jesus fell three times, how Veronica wiped his face, how Simon helped carry his cross, and how his mother, Mary, cried upon seeing him. I think about the sorrows of the world, in Rwanda, Somalia, Haiti, or Iraq, and I wonder what I can do about it.

As I hear Jesus' last testimony—words like "Father, forgive them; for they do not know what they do" and "Father, into Your hands I commend My spirit"—I am reminded that this world and all of its suffering are not permanent, and that there is something beyond all the appointments scheduled on my day-planner to hope for and to live for. I breathe a sigh of relief that I will not ultimately be judged on the patterned drapes I didn't sew for my son's room, or the delicious meals I didn't cook for my husband, or even the number of hours I didn't spend volunteering on the parish council.

Every year, the stations are the same—Jesus always meets the women of Jerusalem; he is always stripped of his garments; he is always nailed to the

cross. I'm comforted by a little repetition and sameness in a rapidly changing world; I relish the sense of
continuity amid confusion that the stations provide.

But each year, the stations also mean something
different. I'm at a different place. As a young mother
of a boy, I better understand the pangs of sorrow
Mary must have felt seeing her son ridiculed,
scourged, and ultimately crucified. As a friend of
someone losing her mother or caring for a sister with
cancer, I try to be Veronica offering even a sliver of
consolation.

The falls in my life change as my priorities shift. I
know when I've failed to be a patient mom, a compassionate wife, and a loyal friend. I cry out Jesus'
familiar words, "My God, my God, why have you
forsaken me?" and demand an explanation from the
Big Guy for all the frustrations of the past year.

And when I stand with the disciples at the tomb,
I'm anxiously awaiting something new—confirmation that I'm sending my son to the right preschool,
an exciting book contract to land on my desk, an
extra shipment of patience from the heavenly store,

the magical lottery ticket to pay off all my bills, or simply the courage and strength to be a better person.

Depending on the year's events, I meditate on each station and pray a certain intention. And then, when I reach the end of the story—the Resurrection—I experience a kind of hope, a hope that is possible because I have not forgotten. I have remembered.

St. Joseph

PAUL MARIANI is a poet, critic, essayist, and biographer of William Carlos Williams, Hart Crane, John Berryman, and Robert Lowell. His latest book is *Thirty Days: On Retreat with the Exercises of St. Ignatius*. Mr. Mariani taught for many years at the University of Massachusetts at Amherst, and he now holds a chair in English at Boston College. He and his wife, Eileen, live in Montague, Massachusetts, and are the parents of three adult sons.

....

My fascination with St. Joseph begins with a story my wife told me forty years ago. It's the story of our first meeting, in a bar off Jericho Turnpike in Mineola, Long Island. She had gone there as a member of a St. John's University sorority,

41

and I too had gone, a recent initiate into Manhattan College's own version of Animal House. A Friday night in mid-December: cold, clear, a few stars flickering in the arc of the yellow streetlights. Eileen had gone with a girlfriend.

Over a beer and a Coke she told me a few bad jokes (her father's specialty, it turned out), and at some point, she says, she signaled to her girlfriend that this one was hers. She left to "freshen up," but really, as she told me years later, to pray to St. Joseph, thus finishing up the ninth and final night of a novena she had promised the saint because she was looking for a guy with at least some reliability. She was all of eighteen, I nineteen.

Over the years, I've seen St. Joseph called on to perform all sorts of ad hoc miracles. Friends—Catholic and non-Catholic—have buried statues of the saint upside down on their property to help sell their homes. Joseph is asked to secure a job, to settle family squabbles. There's St. Joseph Aspirin—baby aspirin, orange, candylike—named for the saint who was the child Jesus' protector and guardian. There's a

St. Joseph River in Michigan and a town called St. Joseph in both Michigan and Missouri. There are the Josephites and the Sisters of St. Joseph, who bathe and feed my wife's ninety-three-year-old widowed mother in their nursing home. And there are hundreds of Catholic schools and colleges and universities and institutes and hospitals and churches named after this silent saint, this shadow of the Father.

Joseph is one of those figures in the Bible without a speaking part. Not a single word, except for the implied *fiat* to God's word played out again and again. What you get instead is a dreamer, a good man—the Bible calls him "just"—someone who seems to have paid attention to what God had planned for him. We learn from the elaborate genealogies that Matthew and Luke give us (both different in their particulars) that Joseph (a common enough name in first-century Palestine) was a *tekton* (in the Greek) or *faber* (in the Latin), that is, a carpenter or worker in wood or stone, from the butt-end-of-jokes hillbilly village of Nazareth, and that he was somehow descended from the great house of

David. Which tells us—if it tells us anything—just how far downhill that lineage had fallen one thousand years after David ruled Israel. In retrospect one sees it as all part of God's gracious design, this taking the lowly of this world and raising them to unheard-of new heights. His plan. His way of proceeding. Certainly not anything Herod or Caesar or even we could have dreamed up.

Joseph, engaged to a young girl from the village, finding her pregnant, tries to figure out how to divorce her quietly, without exposing her shame—that is, without having Mary publicly stoned to death for the crime of adultery. And then comes a dream, a dream in which Joseph hears an angel telling him not to be afraid to take Mary into his home, that this child is different, that the father of this child is God, working through the Holy Spirit, and that this child is destined "to save people from their sins." And Joseph does what the angel has commanded him to do and takes the young woman into his home and becomes the child's father. Of course there are the jokes at Joseph's expense one finds in literature: in James Joyce's *Ulysses,* for instance, which is a book about fatherhood ("it was the pigeon, Joseph"), or in William Carlos Williams's *Paterson,* with its image of the "pot-bellied/graybeard" in Pieter Brueghel's sixteenth-century painting *The Adoration of the Kings.* But what all such jokes really tell us is that the profane imagination seems balked by the mystery of the sacred, the human imagination falling away from the fact of the divine imagination Wording things as it wills.

For fifteen centuries—except here and there—Joseph was pretty much overlooked, though you get early (tenth-century) images of a young man watching over his wife and baby, and—half a millennium later—Joseph as an old man with a bald pate, a safe enough figure to guard Mary's virginity; it is important, though, to remember that the biblical Joseph was accepted as Jesus' father in Nazareth, and so must have been a virile enough figure to stop the wagging tongues of a small village. In time, as the human imagination became more and more interested in the history of the human Jesus, so too did it become interested in the human figure of Joseph. Which was why he was painted by—among so many others—Filippo Lippi, Giotto, Perugino, Bellini, Veronese, Dossi, Giorgione, Andrea del Sarto, Raphael, Michelangelo, Titian, and Poussin.

Each year on March 19, Catholics celebrate the Feast of St. Joseph, though here in the United States Joseph is often overshadowed by the festivities surrounding St. Patrick, whether you're Irish or not. The other important day in the calendar for Joseph is May 1—May Day—when Joseph is celebrated as patron of workers, a memorial set up originally to counterbalance the Communist worker parades on that day, much—I suppose—as a December Christmas was instituted to supplant the pagan festivities of the winter Saturnalia. And in the mid–nineteenth century it was Leo XIII who proclaimed Joseph patron of the universal church, a sort of culmination of the saint's earlier patronage of individual countries, like Mexico, Canada, Bohemia, and Belgium.

It is easy to overlook Joseph, much as we overlook those millions of men and women who do their work quietly and well, without the least fanfare, and who for the most part never make the papers. And it is just this sense of anonymity, of invisibility, that attracts me to him: that he was a good provider, that he was chosen to care for God's only son, to watch over him, teach him, shape him, and to protect and love the boy's mother. One can only guess what they in their turn did for him. A man without a passport or influential friends, he had to move about in a world without safety nets of any sort (except for those you couldn't put a finger on), a world of assassins and government killers and psychotics and informants, a world overseen by a foreign power that could—when it wanted to—move swiftly to squelch anything that smacked of rebellion or cross-purposes.

For me, then, watching the ways in which my sons confide in their mother, with her understanding and quiet wisdom, and finding myself still aching for all of them, mother and sons—even now, when two of my boys are married and the other is a Jesuit priest preparing for the missions—I appreciate even more Joseph's unobtrusive, necessary role in salvation history. I think of him teaching his young son how to follow the grain of a piece of olive wood, how to plane it, learning patience, trying to earn a fair day's wages for a fair day's work to put that daily bread on the table. Or perhaps patiently standing in a queue, looking for work. I think of Joseph—to paraphrase the Jesuit poet Gerard Manley Hopkins—living in ten thousand places: in the man rising at 2:00 A.M. to plow the deserted snow-clogged roads, the nurse working the night shift and then a day shift, the cop on the lonely beat, the mother with the autistic daughter or paralyzed son, the office worker biting his lip at some slight or racial insensitivity against him, because he too has bread to put on his family's table. I think of him as someone with photos of his wife and kid hanging on the wall behind his cubicle, telling me that—as much as he'd like to sell me another car—I can still get another couple of years out of the one I've got. The thousand daily human gestures of a man going about his rounds each day. But a dreamer too, dreaming dreams in which he hears voices, as once he believed he'd heard a voice that loved and trusted him enough to place a son— and the son's mother—in his faltering, capable, and very human hands.

Lectio Divina

DANIEL J. HARRINGTON, S.J., is a Jesuit priest and professor of New Testament at Weston Jesuit School of Theology in Cambridge, Massachusetts. An internationally recognized Scripture scholar, Fr. Harrington is the editor of the journal *New Testament Abstracts* and the *Sacra Pagina* series of books. He is the author of numerous scholarly articles and books, including *Interpreting the New Testament* and *Why Do We Suffer?* and is a former president of the Catholic Biblical Association of America.

....

*L*ectio divina is Latin for "spiritual reading." It is a method of reading and praying on Scripture and other classics of spirituality like Augustine's *Confessions* and *The Imitation of Christ*. It has deep roots in the history of monasticism. There are four basic steps in *lectio divina:* reading (What does this text say?), meditation (What does this text say to me?), prayer (What do I want to say to God through this text?), and contemplation or action (What difference might this text make in my life?).

The text to be read can be long or short. And the full process of "reading" could take fifteen minutes or be spread over fifteen years. To illustrate the process, I will focus on Jesus' invitation in Mt 11:28: "Come to me, all you who are weary and carrying heavy burdens, and I will give you rest."

Reading *(lectio)* the text involves basic literary analysis—that is, looking at its context, words and images, characters, literary form and structure. Here Jesus issues an invitation to come to his wisdom school and promises both wisdom and rest to those who accept. The saying is part of a passage (Mt 11:25–30) that reveals Jesus as both the Son of God and incarnate wisdom in a context (Mt chaps. 11–12) where the themes of unbelief and rejection are prominent. One's appreciation of Jesus' invitation and promise grows when the passage is read along-side Jer 6:16 ("where the good way lies . . . walk in it, and find rest for your souls") and Sir 51:26–27 ("put your neck under her [Wisdom's] yoke. . . . I have labored little and found much serenity").

Meditation *(meditatio)* takes account of both the content of the passage and the present dispositions of the reader. Many rich theological themes emerge from Mt 11:28: real wisdom as divine revelation, the human search for wisdom and "rest," Jesus as a gentle and humble teacher, Jesus as wisdom incarnate, and so on.

What this text says to me will also depend to some extent on my state of soul as I read it. I may be tired, discouraged, and depressed, and so badly in need of "rest." Or I may be feeling wonderful, hoping for a new breakthrough on the way of wisdom and more convinced than ever that true wisdom is to be found only in the teaching and example of Jesus.

Prayer *(oratio)* flows from reading and meditating on the text. This step, of course, is very personal. I may ask God for peace of soul. Or I may praise God for the gift of faith and the wisdom of Jesus. Or I may thank God for having revealed himself in and through Jesus to "little ones."

The fourth step may take the form of *contemplatio* (relishing the spiritual experience and praising God for it) or *actio* (discerning some course of action). For example, through Mt 11:28 I may decide to devote myself to learning more about the wisdom of Jesus. Or I may determine to make a retreat or to pray more regularly. Or I may just take a vacation, or at least try to grasp what the "rest" that Jesus promises means for how I live and work.

Lectio divina is profoundly simple and eminently flexible. While rooted in monastic practice, it is also part of the larger heritage of Christian spirituality. It can help greatly in integrating biblical scholarship and the devotional life. It can be used with Ignatian contemplation (application of the senses and identification with the characters), especially in *meditatio*.

For individuals and groups just beginning the practice of *lectio divina,* it may be wise to follow the four-step outline rather mechanically. But I must confess that I now seldom consciously work through the various steps all in one time period. In fact, the point of *lectio divina* is to foster an immersion in Scripture so that the various questions arise naturally in their own time. For one who has been privileged to study, teach, and write about Scripture for many years, the framework has become so habitual that eventually all the steps get covered in one way or another. A wise teacher once told me, "When you have mastered a method or skill, then you can throw away the instruction booklet."

The fathers of the church originated *lectio divina,* with Jerome especially giving it structure. Benedict incorporated it into his monastic rule, and in the twelfth century Guigo II (the ninth prior of the Grande Chartreuse monastery) wrote an important letter on it titled "The Ladder of Monks."

While *lectio divina* has never disappeared from the Christian tradition since patristic times, it has undergone a revival in large part through the recently retired archbishop of Milan, Cardinal Carlo Maria Martini, S.J. A distinguished biblical scholar and former rector of the Pontifical Biblical Institute in Rome, Martini used *lectio divina* as a pastoral tool in his archdiocese and in his many books. Through Martini's imaginative leadership, *lectio divina* has become available to everyone, not only for private devotions but also for communal Bible studies, prayer groups, and liturgical activities.

If we are committed to the mandates of the Second Vatican Council to make Scripture the soul of theology and to become a more biblical church, *lectio divina* can be an effective tool, tested by hundreds of years of experience. It is another case of bringing out of our biblical treasure "what is new and what is old" (Mt 13:52). While *lectio divina* is old, its use as a pastoral tool for the whole church is new and promising.

Holy Water

ANN WROE is special features editor at *The Economist* and a regular columnist for the *Tablet*. Formerly the literary editor of *The Economist,* she is also the author of the award-winning biography *Pontius Pilate,* and *The Perfect Prince,* about a fifteenth-century claimant to the English throne. Ms. Wroe lives in London with her husband, three teenage sons, and, as she says, a "crazed dog."

....

I have never felt the attachment I should to the daily prayers of the church. Their depth and meaning have rubbed off with repetition, to the point where I am stirred by them only when I say them in a foreign language. Words are tricky that way.

It is very different with my favorite ritual, which is carried out in silence: the taking of holy water at the door of the church.

There is, I know, nothing particularly Catholic or even Christian about this action: the taking of water to sanctify and purify is a ritual almost as old as mankind. Britain and Ireland are dotted with springs and wells that have been sacred successively to Celts, Romans, medieval hermits, and modern schoolchildren. Some are still overshadowed by their holy trees—oaks, hawthorn, ash, and yew—on which visitors hang little scraps of cloth, or into whose bark they press coins in the hope of healing.

Such practices may be dismissed as pagan, but they do not seem so to me. Water and trees have a deep symbolism to Christians, too, as instruments of our salvation. That is why I have sometimes felt moved to make the sign of the cross in the middle of a wood or at the sight of a solitary tree, and why, coming up on a spring rising by the side of the road or on a hillside, I almost always do so.

Holy-water stoups came very early to Christianity. Stoups of marble, glass, and terra cotta have been found in the catacombs, and niches and urns for water occur in ancient cemeteries as well as churches. Many holy-water fonts were simple, sometimes no more than seashells; others were grand affairs, proper fountains for ablutions of both hands and feet. A visitor to St. Sophia in sixth-century Constantinople described water "gurgling noisily into the air" from a bronze pipe "with a force that banishes all evils." Medieval stoups were sometimes segregated, with nobles dipping their hands in one and the unwashed in another.

We no longer use the font to wash, but taking water upon entering a church is still a vital act. It recognizes the demarcation between secular and sacred space: we have turned out of the noisy street into God's quiet place, and we acknowledge it. We also remember our baptism, our entry by water into the larger church; but this time we perform the sacrament ourselves, in miniature. And we purify ourselves for spiritual action, even if it is only the action of sitting in silence for a while or looking at the stained glass. I daresay there are prayers to accompany the action, but I myself never say any. The action, in fact, empties my mind of the words that constantly teem there—empties it long enough, perhaps, to prepare myself to be silent and listen.

I feel cheated if, on entering a church, the stoup is dry. It happens disappointingly often: dust on the fingertips, or a tide line of green mold where life and spirit should be. Whenever this occurs, I find it hard to settle. My prayer itself seems dry, as if water is the medium that makes it work. Our local priest once explained that he could not fill the stoup because he had no water that had been blessed. But I feel that all water is blessed, even six-times-recycled London water from the tap, and I fetched some from the sanctuary to make the point. The action of making the sign of the cross with water is wonderfully strengthening and restoring, no matter how humble its origins; just as a glass of this water, if you are truly thirsty, refreshes the parched body as well as any other.

It also seems important that I do the action for myself. I have always felt a little doubtful about the ritual of asperging. Most priests I know do it with joyful, almost childlike, abandon, but the water falls too haphazardly, as if never meant for me in the first place. There is more benediction in walking through a shower of rain: rain falling softly and evenly on both the just and the unjust, the best metaphor for the mercy of God. Rather than accept the dubious blessing chance throws me, I must deliberately and consciously take up the drops myself. It is a sanctification that links me to every man and woman who has ever felt God through water, and thanked him, a line of wordless prayer that goes back almost to the dawn of humankind itself.

The Rosary

SALLY CUNNEEN is the author of a number of books, including *In Search of Mary: The Woman and the Symbol* and *Mother Church: What the Experience of Women Is Teaching Her.* She is a cofounder of *Cross Currents* magazine and a professor emeritus at Rockland Community College of the State University of New York. Ms. Cunneen and her husband, Joseph, live in West Nyack, New York, and are the parents of three adult sons.

....

The Rosary is the oldest and most popular of all private Catholic devotions, and one that has been strongly promoted by the church since the fifteenth century. The origin of bead circlets used to aid in prayerful meditation is lost in ancient Eastern customs—the Chinese Kwan Yin statue in my living room wears such a circlet of beads—but they were certainly used in the early Middle Ages by Christian believers, who counted them praying the Our Father, the Hail Mary, and the Glory Be as they meditated. Not until the thirteenth century, however, at the height of European Marian devotion, was such a circlet called a "Rosary," making it a spiritual bouquet named for Mary's flower.

When most Christians were illiterate and when books, including Bibles, were unavailable except in monasteries, a string of beads or seeds provided a simple means for the faithful to re-create their attachment to the events of the Gospel as they prayed the prayer that Jesus taught and, also, repeated the words of Gabriel and Elizabeth to Mary. By the sixteenth century the mysteries were standardized and minimized to the fifteen we all know: the joyful (the Annunciation, the Visitation, the Nativity, the Presentation, and the Finding of the Child Jesus); the sorrowful (the Agony in the Garden, the Scourging, the Crowning with Thorns, the Carrying of the Cross, and the Death of Jesus); and the glorious (the Resurrection, the Ascension, the Descent of the Holy Spirit upon the Apostles, the Assumption, and the Coronation of Mary).

But in 2002 Pope John Paul II put his imprint on the Rosary, as he has on so much else, bringing it to the front pages when he added a fourth set of mysteries: the mysteries of light, or "luminous" mysteries. These focus largely on Christ's life related to the sacraments of the church: the Baptism of Jesus, the Wedding Feast at Cana, the Proclamation of the Kingdom of God, the Transfiguration, and the Institution of the Eucharist. Teachers, Rosary societies, and the faithful in general are now mulling over the meaning of these additions. Tentatively they seem to balance an overemphasis on Marian devotions in the first fifteen mysteries. This is especially interesting from a pope who is so devoted to Mary, and suggests that he sees her as the Second Vatican Council did, firmly within the community of the church.

But except when it is said in groups and at official functions, the Rosary remains a private devotion, aimed at meditation. And as such, for many twenty-first-century believers, it poses some problems. Is it in fact possible both to say the prayers and to meditate on the mysteries? Some are able to say the words as they move their fingers on the beads without concentrating on them as a kind of mantra that frees the mind to focus on the mysteries. But from my own experience and observation, many people cannot. The majority no longer pray the Rosary as their mothers and grandmothers did. It is still taught in Catholic schools, particularly in October and May, Mary's months, but not automatically included in daily prayers, as it was in my childhood.

For those seriously interested in meditation today, many books and meditative paths are available. And it is no secret that a great many serious practitioners of contemplative prayer do not say the Rosary, for it blocks the simpler, higher prayer they have learned to engage in. Here, for instance, is the confession of a doctor of the church, St. Thérèse of Lisieux:

When alone (I am ashamed to admit it) the recitation of the rosary is more difficult for me than the wearing of an instrument of penance. . . . I force myself in vain to meditate on the mysteries of the rosary; I don't succeed in fixing my mind on them. . . . I think that the Queen of heaven, since she is *my Mother,* must see my good will and she is satisfied with it.[1]

Nevertheless, the Rosary has served many purposes and many different sorts of people over the centuries and continues to do so. Like most such devotional aids, it can be reduced to rote or become a springboard to the conversation with God it aims to induce. It is still widely used in regular prayer sessions, in groups, and, in whole or in part, by many Catholics in time of danger, worry, or grief. Though I share Thérèse's difficulties and seldom pray a whole Rosary, at trying times I frequently reach out for my mother's beads—given her as a wedding present by my father—and gain some degree of perspective as I return to the old habit.

The Rosary is a far more complex and multi-purpose devotional aid than its simple history and this short description suggest. To be able to hold a real object while praying is not only comforting; it connects me physically and psychologically with the reality of the Incarnation. It is an objective reminder that Christ is present here and now, within me and without. And when I can connect mentally with either the words of the individual prayers or the mysteries, I am also brought into contact with the life and message of Jesus and his followers. Such an experience is very Catholic, very Christian, and truly human.

The Saints

LAWRENCE S. CUNNINGHAM is the John A. O'Brien Professor of Theology at the University of Notre Dame. The author or editor of seventeen books, he has been three times honored by the Catholic Press Association for his popular writing and twice honored with teaching awards at his university. His most recent work is *Thomas Merton and the Monastic Vision,* and he is currently writing a book on the saints as a theological resource. Mr. Cunningham and his wife, Cecilia, are the parents of two adult children, Julia and Sarah, who attend Notre Dame.

....

It always disappoints me a bit when the celebrant at Mass chooses the first eucharistic prayer (the Roman Canon) and skips the invocation of the saints—that resonant list of early martyrs—recited before and after the institutional narrative. The omission is all the more disappointing since one of those lists is made up of heroic women who otherwise are absent in the usual language of the liturgy. While it is true that those names of the saints appear in small print as optional for the celebrant in the sacramentary, what is gained by their omission? Less than a minute would be my guess. My own strong conviction is that within the precise act of naming those saints is an act that goes well beyond ornament and decorum. In fact, that brief calling to mind contains within it, symbolically, a historical reminder of how the cult of the saints got started as well as enunciating a deep theological truth.

Naming the saints within the context of the official prayer of the church—the apex of the church's life as the Second Vatican Council called it—reminds us that as Christians in the here and now, we stand in solidarity with all those who have gone before who live as part of the church itself. It is for that reason that that part of the eucharistic prayer begins "In union with the whole church . . ." as it calls on Mary, Joseph, the apostles, martyrs, and all the saints. We stand with all those who are so named, making up what the epistle to the Hebrews calls "the great cloud of witnesses" (Heb 12:1). The "cloud of witnesses" is the church writ large.

The veneration of the saints began in the Catholic Church with honors paid to those who died for the faith in the Roman persecutions. Veneration of the martyrs can be traced back to the second century, but by the fourth there was already in place a calendar of saints' feast days that honored their *dies natalis* (literally a "birth day," which was the day of their death), liturgical ceremonies, pilgrimages to their burial places, and traditions seeking their intercession. It is worthwhile to remember that well into the Middle Ages the most important honor enjoyed by the popes was in their role as protector and custodian of the tombs of St. Peter and St. Paul.

The naming of the saints in the eucharistic liturgy is not a historical adornment but a theological claim, namely, that the veneration of the saints included those who are not known by name but who "sleep in Christ." The tradition reflects the full sense of the church as a living reality beyond the merely socio-logical and contemporary.

At the end of the Roman persecutions in the early fourth century, the instinct for venerating the saints did not end. The ascetics, monks, great pastoral bishops, holy women and men were honored for their outstanding imitation of Christ and as those who provided the church with new models of holi-ness. St. Athanasius, in his famous book on the monk Anthony, caught the continuity between the old and the new well when he observed that Anthony was a martyr every day of his life. Such out-standing figures were honored in their lifetime and venerated after their death.

In premodern cultures the space between our world and that of the spiritual was extremely porous. Saints were considered not only to be great figures of the faith but also ready aides before the throne of God and powerful conduits of grace, healing, and help. Their relics were loci of power. Their shrines and churches were awesome centers of prayer and places where miracles not only happened but were expected. Pilgrimage to their shrines was a common part of medieval culture and a frequent metaphor for the Christian life itself. Both Dante and Chaucer, in their respective masterworks, set their stories within the language of pilgrimage.

North America, a land of immigrants, reflects in its church life the ancient popular heritage of honoring the saints whose memory has been kept alive as peoples have crossed the ocean to this country. In the medium-sized, blue-collar town where I live this memory is clear, with parishes reflecting the ethnic background of their congregations: for example, St. Patrick (Irish), St. Stephen (Hungarian), St. Adalbert (Polish), St. Augustine (African American), and St. Bavo (Belgian).

This popular tradition of honoring the saints was very much a part of my own upbringing. The nuns in our parochial school told us the stories of the saints that are still part of my memory. We had discussions about what patronal saint's name we would choose for confirmation. We celebrated the Feasts of St. Patrick and St. Joseph in the local parish church. We had our throats blessed on St. Blaise's Day. The side altars of our parish church had candles burning before the statues of St. Anthony (patron of lost things), St. Jude (patron of hopeless cases), and the Little Flower, whose fame was widespread. Each week some men of the parish would meet under the patronage of St. Vincent de Paul to plan their work for the poor of the parish. Altar boys learned of St. Tarcisius, and the priests, always eager to foster vocations, would tell stories of St. John Vianney, the patron saint of parish priests. I knew from a young age that St. Lawrence, the saint for whom I was named, was burned on a griddle by the Romans. Every automobile we owned had a St. Christopher's medal on the dashboard.

The stories we learned by reading or listening were reinforced by a strong visual culture: we *saw* the saints. We had holy cards with pictures of the saints to be tucked into our missals. The stained-glass windows taught us a saintly vocabulary: Sebastian with his arrow-studded body; Catherine with her wheel; Barbara with her tower; the Little Flower with her shower of rose petals; Francis showing the wounds in his hands; Peter with his keys and Paul his sword. Our classroom bulletin boards never lacked a saint's saying and a picture.

What is interesting about the contemporary church in which we live is that the kinds of saints we are interested in are not always those who are canonized. Countless are the many works of mercy placed under the patronage of Peter Maurin and Dorothy Day. Innumerable are the young people who are inspired to work with the poor because of Oscar Romero or the martyred women and men in Central and Latin America. Countless are those who seek a deeper life of prayer because of the writings of Thomas Merton.

With the search for saintly models for our time— a search amply aided by the papal interest in saints—come a new vocabulary and a new iconography. The ancient martyrs died out of hatred for the faith; many of today's martyrs die because of a hatred for love and charity. We live in an odd age, when people who claim to be Christians by heritage mercilessly persecute other Christians out of hatred for their social ideas and activities. More than likely, every one of the trigger men who, in 1989, shot the Salvadoran Jesuits and their companions was a baptized Catholic. The old iconography of martyrdom featured lions, the executioner's axe, or the burning pyre. Today's iconography must show the gas chamber, the bullet in the back of the head, and the torturer's electrodes. The vocabulary and the iconography change, but the story of martyrdom remains the same.

It is difficult to generalize about how contemporary Catholics view the saints. Many still invoke them for help, as the crowds of international visitors who line up to pray before the altar of Blessed John XXIII in St. Peter's Basilica attest. Others—perhaps a majority—seek in our saints models of how to be a Christian in this age. Pope John Paul II frequently alludes to the martyrs in his writings for the simple reason that those witnesses show that there are some things that are so valuable and true that it is a worthy thing to say so with one's life. The tradition of the saints is a long meditation (a kind of existential exegesis) on the Word of God. It was the late Karl Rahner, S.J., who wrote that the saint is the person who shows us that in *this* particular way it is possible to be a Christian.

Finally, I come back to the liturgy. The invocation of the saints in our common worship reminds us of the capacious character of the church, which, as the patristic tradition loves to say, reaches back into the just men and women of the Old Testament, continues through the Christian tradition, and includes us in this day and age. The church is one vast *ekklesia* of the living and the dead mutually supporting each other by our common prayer to the Father with Christ in the Spirit. In that great democracy the saints we call by name and those unnamed whom we remember are not figures frozen in glass or carved from stone but brothers and sisters. Not to understand that is to live with an emaciated and impoverished understanding of the church.

The liturgical honor paid to the saints has a strong eschatological edge to it. We hope to be what they are: those who now see the face of God. Under that umbrella of God's presence are not only those who are named in the canon of those officially recognized by the church but all those who "sleep in Christ." To honor the saints is to honor all those of our own families who are with the Lord. It is also a yearning that we too will be with them when we die as we are imperfectly with them as we keep their memories alive. In the reading in the breviary for the Feast of All Saints, St. Bernard of Clairvaux makes that point explicitly. Here is what he says to his twelfth-century monastic audience: "We long to share in the citizenship of heaven, to dwell with the spirits of the blessed, to join the assembly of the patriarchs, the ranks of the prophets, the council of the apostles, the great host of martyrs, the noble company of confessors, and the choir of virgins. In short, we long to be united in happiness with all the saints."

The Miraculous
Medal

ROBERT P. MALONEY, C.M., has been superior general
of the Congregation of the Mission (the Vincentians) for the
past eleven years and resides in Rome. Before his current
position, Fr. Maloney served as pastor in a village in a poor
region of Panama, where he helped to form lay leaders to
conduct Sunday celebrations of the Word and prepare
parishioners for reception of the sacraments. Prior to his time
in Panama, he worked for sixteen years in the formation of
priests in the United States. Fr. Maloney is the author of a
number of books, including *The Way of St. Vincent de Paul*.

....

On the night of July 18, 1830, in a chapel on
Rue du Bac in Paris, Catherine Labouré, a
twenty-four-year-old novice of the Daughters of

Charity, had a vision of the Virgin Mary. They spoke familiarly for two hours. In this conversation, and in a second apparition on November 27, Mary gave Catherine a twofold mission: a medal was to be struck in her honor, and Catherine was to promote youth groups that would wear the medal and serve the poor.

During Catherine's lifetime, more than one billion medals were made and distributed to the remotest corners of the world. Initially, the medal had a special attraction for the poor, who came to call it the "Miraculous Medal." Eventually, countless others from every level of society began to wear it. Born in an era of rationalism, the medal proclaimed the need for symbols to express faith, love, and commitment. The symbols on the medal were, in fact, a graphic catechesis about God's provident care for his people.

Today, here in the United States, more than ten million people wear the medal. Many also frequently pray the Miraculous Medal novena.

The medal depicts Mary standing on a globe, with her foot crushing a serpent's head. From her hands beam forth rays of grace. Twelve stars, recalling the woman of the Apocalypse (Rv 12:1) who conquered evil, encircle her head. Inscribed around the edge of the medal's face are the words "O Mary, conceived without sin, pray for us who have recourse to thee." On the reverse, the hearts of Jesus and Mary stand out in relief: his crowned with thorns, hers pierced with a sword. They symbolize the centrality of suffering love in the Gospels. A cross lies above these hearts, linked with the letter *M* to indicate Mary's participation in the mystery of Jesus' death. Once again the twelve stars appear.

Every era rereads the Gospel. It must do so if God's word is to remain alive. So it is too with Marian doctrine, which has developed over the centuries, with strikingly new emphases in different ages. In John's Gospel, Mary is the "Mother of Jesus." Believers in the second and third centuries, reflecting on the Old Testament, recognized her as the "new Eve." In the fourth and fifth centuries, in the midst of turbulent christological heresies, the church solemnly proclaimed Mary as "Mother of God." Subsequent eras identified her as the "Sorrowful

Mother," the "Black Madonna," the "Immaculate Conception," the "Queen of Heaven." Our own age regards her in a renewed way as the "Mother of the Church" and the "Mother of the Poor."

Today many are rereading the Miraculous Medal with a focus on Mary as Mother of the Poor. While the medal's message is relevant for all, it is especially so for those who are marginalized. In this light, how can devotion to the Miraculous Medal take on new meaning in the United States today?

For one thing, Marian devotion occupies an enormous place in the religious culture of the tens of millions of people who continue to flock to the United States: Latin Americans, Filipinos, Vietnamese, and many other immigrant groups.

The most obvious challenge of the medal—not only for these new refugees but also for many of us whose families immigrated generations ago—is to emulate Mary, the first, the preeminent disciple. I would suggest that the medal challenges its more than ten million wearers in the United States to have, like Mary, three characteristics:

To be faithful listeners to God's word. The Gospels present Mary as the model for all believers. Beyond all others, she knew how to "listen to the word of God and act upon it" (Lk 8:21). On the deepest level, those who wear the medal are making a statement: I commit myself to live like Mary and to listen attentively each day to what God is saying to me.

To be faith-filled pray-ers. In a frantically busy, seemingly self-sufficient world, quiet prayer is extremely important. The poet Tennyson wrote, "More things are wrought by prayer than this world dreams of." The message that the Miraculous Medal shouts out to the world is this: Prayer is essential; those who ask, receive; those who seek, find; to those who knock, the door is opened.

To live in solidarity with the poor. Mary lives in solidarity with the poor of Israel. In fact, she is their spokesperson in the Gospels. She cries out in gratitude to God for his many gifts: "My soul proclaims the greatness of the Lord. My spirit rejoices in God my Savior" (Lk 1:46–47). And she recognizes that God can turn the world upside down: "He casts down the mighty from their thrones and lifts up the lowly" (Lk 1:52). In 1830, Mary, through Catherine Labouré, called young people to stand in solidarity with society's poorest. This message is all the more relevant today, when the church proclaims Mary as Mother of the Poor.

Catherine Labouré was a precursor. The medal that flowed from her visions gave popular expression and powerful impetus to the dogma of the Immaculate Conception, which Pius IX proclaimed two decades later in 1854. Surely without Catherine, Christians throughout the world would never have prayed so often, "O Mary, conceived without sin, pray for us who have recourse to thee."

Pilgrimage

KEVIN WHITE, S.J., was ordained a Jesuit priest in 1999 after completing his licentiate in sacred theology at Weston Jesuit School of Theology in Cambridge, Massachusetts. Before joining the Society of Jesus he worked for two years with the Peace Corps in Kenya and also received a master's degree in public policy from the University of Michigan. Fr. White, forty-one, is currently a theology teacher and campus minister at Boston College High School.

....

A mong the gifts I received upon my ordination to the priesthood, one that has proved unexpectedly valuable is the *Book of Blessings*. Its prayers bring to bear on all moments of life the wisdom of Scripture and tradition. I realized this when searching for fitting words to begin our pilgrimage to World Youth Day in 2002.

During the previous school year at Boston College High School, another Jesuit and I encouraged students to join us for two weeks of pilgrimage in Canada. After months of publicity, planning, and begging for funds, six students and the two of us, after an early July morning Mass, climbed into our school van to begin our pilgrimage, prepared with these apt words from my *Book of Blessings:*

> Brothers, as we set out, we should remind ourselves of the reasons for our resolve to go on this holy pilgrimage. The place we intend to visit is a monument to the devotion of the people of God. They have gone there in great numbers to be strengthened in the Christian way of life and to become more determined to devote themselves to the works of charity. We must also try to bring something to the faithful who live there: our example of faith, hope, and love. In this way both they and we will be enriched by the help we give each other.[1]

The human heart naturally seeks God. Consequently, pilgrimages to memorials of God's saving presence have been and remain universal expressions of this deep yearning. Christian Scripture attests to this fact. In the Old Testament, we read that Abraham and Jacob memorialized encounters with God, who had committed himself to care and fidelity, while they set off in faith to the Promised Land (Gn 12:6–7, 28:10–22). Mount Sinai became the destination for the freed tribes of Israel after the Exodus (Ex 19–20). Once settled in the Promised Land, Jerusalem with its ark and temple became the object of obligatory pilgrimage. Indeed, Psalms 120 to 134 were hymns sung by pilgrims as they went up to the holy city.

The New Testament also records numerous pilgrimages. Joseph and Mary were separated from the young Jesus while on pilgrimage to Jerusalem (Lk 2:41–45); Jesus journeyed as a pilgrim to Jerusalem frequently to celebrate the liturgical feasts (Jn 2:13, 5:1, 12:20); Christ suffered, died, and rose again during a time of pilgrimage (Mt 26:17; Mk 14:12;

Lk 22:7–8; Jn 13:1); and the outpouring of the Spirit that formed the church descended on gathered pilgrims (Acts 2:1–11). Pilgrimages are indeed occasions for grace.

The chronicle of Christian pilgrimages is rich in grace, history, and evangelization. So too was ours. We set off that July morning for the Jesuit Martyrs' Shrine in Midland, Ontario, where we joined a thousand other pilgrims from Jesuit schools around the world for a week of formation in Ignatian spirituality. We slept in huge tents, ate meals in fields, prayed outdoors, and visited ground hallowed by the labor, prayer, and blood of earlier Jesuits and their companions on fire with the gospel. We followed the World Youth Day cross to Toronto for another week of prayer and activities with hundreds of thousands of other pilgrims from around the world—a powerful sign of the church's universality and vitality. We lodged in a school-turned-hostel for six hundred pilgrims from Boston, New Orleans, Paris, and Versailles. "Father," one student remarked, realizing that his foreign language study back in Boston was more than an elaborate fabrication, "these people really speak French. Like, they say *'Bonjour'* in the morning."

When I recently asked our students to recall highlights of the pilgrimage, they mentioned meeting fellow Catholics from around the world enthusiastic in their faith; praying in many languages; the graced (my word, not theirs) hardships of irregular sleep, cold showers, passable food, heat, sun, rain, mud, and mosquitoes; the stirring Way of the Cross performed in the streets of Toronto; and the papal Mass at which Pope John Paul II challenged all eight hundred thousand of us rain-soaked and mud-covered pilgrims to be light and salt for the world in the third millennium. The extraordinary generosity of people, especially our Jesuit hosts along the way, was also on their list.

Aside from reserving dates for the next World Youth Day, how can pilgrimage be a part of one's more ordinary devotional life? Set out for a distant shrine, or even a neighboring church. Pray for an intention along the way, and allow for some hardship, some lessening of control. Self-denial is as fundamental to pilgrimage as it is to authentic Christian living. Beware of any spirituality that does not ask something of you. St. Ignatius of Loyola, who called himself "the pilgrim," required pilgrimages of all aspirants to his order to foster reliance on our Creator and Lord (*General Examen,* no. 67). Keep this wisdom in mind. Upon arrival, return to the Lord through the sacrament of reconciliation and resolve to donate income or time to those in special need.

At the end of our pilgrimage, weary and weathered, we gathered again in our school's chapel and, opening the *Book of Blessings,* I found the perfect prayer to conclude our pilgrimage to Canada and to set out again on our more ordinary, daily discipleship:

> Blessed are you, O God, Father of our Lord Jesus Christ. From all races of the earth you have chosen a people dedicated to you, eager to do what is right. Your grace has moved our hearts to love you more deeply and to serve you more generously. Bless us so that we may tell of your wonderful deeds and give proof of them in our lives. We ask this through Christ our Lord. Amen.[2]

Litanies

WILLIAM GRIFFIN is an author, editor, journalist, anthologist, and translator. During his twenty years with major American publishing houses, he acquired and edited over five hundred books. Mr. Griffin has written biographies on C. S. Lewis and Billy Graham, and has translated, among other works, Thomas à Kempis's *Imitation of Christ* and *Soliloquy of a Soul,* as well as St. Augustine's *Confessions* and *Sermons to the People: Advent, Christmas, New Year's, Epiphany*. He and his wife, Emilie, are the parents of three adult children and live in Alexandria, Louisiana.

....

By the time of Gregory the Great (d. 604), the Litany of the Saints, first of the great Latin litanies, was a full-blown, dress-up affair. Best vestments and all of that. Copes and chasubles. Embroidered and brocaded. Nauters and thurifers. Obviously, it was a prayer for the clergy; they shared with the choir and later with the congregation, but only in an antiphonal way. That is to say, the clergy led; the choir and/or congregation followed as the procession rolled down a street or padded around a church.

Despite such extravagant beginnings, the litany eventually petered down to a more private devotion, at least among certain religious communities. When I was a member of the Society of Jesus from 1952 to 1960, happy days all, the last item posted on the *ordo diei* was *Litaniae*—in the plural because the Jesuits had intertwined the Litany of the Saints with the Litany of the Blessed Virgin Mary; in Latin because, well, the litany was composed in Latin and was still said or sung in Latin at that time.

A house bell was rung at 8:55 P.M. for the litanies at 9:00. Two hundred of us assembled in the chapel, and the designated priest walked down to the front, flopped on the prie-dieu, began to recite the litany, and we responded after every invocation.

Now during a liturgy the chanting of a litany was always slow, stately, gorgeous. But as a private devotion it could become fast, scattered, riotous. In fact, we used to joke that the designated priest on many a night could be called "Fr. Jack D. Ripper, S.J." The faster he "ripped" through the repetitions, the more he was esteemed, at least by the younger members of the community. The night he broke the ten-minute barrier for the twenty-minute prayer there was a murmur of awe. When the seven-minute barrier finally fell, we felt we were in the presence of greatness. Alas, the fictional father has gone to his reward, and the *Litaniae* have disappeared from the Jesuits' daily community devotions. But for some reason as yet unknown to me, they've remained a firm and indeed warm part of mine.

My point is that you needn't just listen to the chanting of a litany in a church or its recitation in a chapel. You may read it by yourself or with a few others. On each successive reading, you and your partners in prayer will find an easy cadence. Perhaps not the thrilling, ethereal renditions of the monks at

Solemnes. Perhaps a more down-to-earth, skip-rope-jingle movement of invocation and response. As for the words of the litany, the invocations move from hierarchy to lowerarchy. From the Trinity, Mary, angels, apostles, evangelists, disciples, martyrs, doctors of the church, popes, confessors, founders of religious orders, right down to the crazies of the desert in the fourth century, and an assortment of women who were some of the above.

All the Trinity and apostles are invoked individually, but of the other groupings only a few popes, a few confessors, a few martyrs, and so on are named. Respectfully, at the end of each grouping there is an invocation to the group as a whole. Hence, no saint can be said to have escaped our notice or our invocation. The Litany of the Saints, as well as many subsequent litanies—Loretto (1587), Marian (from 1297 on), Holy Name (1862), Sacred Heart (1899), St. Joseph (1909), Most Precious Blood (1960)—has been approved and indulgenced for public recitation in churches. But when said privately by yourself or with others, a litany, any litany, is also a festoonable prayer. You can customize it any way you want.

Here are some suggestions with regard to the Litany of the Saints.

First, the saints mentioned by name, as well as the petitions urged on the Almighty during the litany, are pitifully few in number. Favorite saints can be added. Certainly more saintly women should be summoned up. (Redress of hot contemporary issues could also be petitioned.)

Second, you could invite some of your curious non-Catholic friends to join you when you pray the litany in English. Surely the Mere Christian, the Common Christian, the Anonymous Christian, the Seminal Christian would not put up too much of a scuffle before partaking in this historical prayer.

Of course, in the litany there's the odd reference to pontiffs but, thankfully, no references to the odd pontiffs. But I'd just as soon leave them all in; church history is church history, for better or worse. But one might also want to substitute, for the response *ora/orate pro nobis* ("pray for us"), the ecumenical variant *ora/orate cum nobis* ("pray with us").

Third, it seems right, meet, and just to include in any ecumenical litany the Protestant reformers as well as the Catholic reformers. Hence, Loyola, Bellarmine, Canisius, and Borromeo could be followed by Calvin, Knox, Luther, and the Wesleys.

Fourth, the Roman Catholic Church has generally preferred its saints to be both dead as doornails *and* dead as doornails for a suitable number of years—say, a century or two—before proclaiming a man or woman as a saint to the world at large. But what about living saints? Risky business, this! By definition, saints are also sinners, and they sin right up until they've breathed their last. Hence, perhaps better to leave out the living.

On the other hand, the apostle Paul, when dictating his encyclicals, often used as a synonym for *Christians* or *believers* the word *saints*. For him saints were the living human beings who had to survive in a pagan world that often was unjust, unrighteous, unsympathetic. And, as in Rom 1:6–7, he used *saints* to address the Christian residents in a certain place. So include the living, but only at your own risk.

All this having been said, what effect does the homely hyssoping of the heavens have to do with the divine economy of things? Well, all I know is that I find the parade, the procession of the saints in a litany, especially an expanded litany, to be something like the communion of saints ball. I invoke each saint's name as he or she comes down the nave, each wearing the costume and carrying the symbol of his or her identity as private person and public saint. Rather a formal affair, yes, but I've read enough hagiography in my lifetime that I also see the saints in their jammies, as it were. No man is a hero to his valet, runs the saw; and no woman to her upstairs maid. Which means, at least in my eyes, the saints were just blokes like the rest of us, schlepping along as best they could. Looked at in this light, they have set me a very good example, and I hasten to keep up.

Mary

JOAN CHITTISTER, O.S.B., is a Benedictine sister and the author of twenty-one books, including *In Search of Belief* and *The Fire in These Ashes: A Spirituality of Contemporary Religious Life.* Sister Joan, a well-known lecturer both in the United States and abroad, is the founder and executive director of Benetvision: A Resource and Research Center for Contemporary Spirituality and has served as president of the Conference of American Benedictine Prioresses and of the Leadership Conference of Women Religious. A theologian, social psychologist, and communication theorist, she has taught on all educational levels and is an active member of the International Peace Council. She lives in a Benedictine community in Erie, Pennsylvania.

....

Perhaps the most revealing thing I can say about Marian devotions is that I myself never had any. At least not for most of my life. In those two statements may lie both the age-old quandary of Mary's place in personal spiritual development and a hint of the continuing impact of Mary of Nazareth throughout the ages.

Mary of Nazareth, as I and my generation received her in the 1950s and 1960s, held no interest for me. She was not my mother's kind of woman. Nor was she the kind of woman my mother was raising *me* to be. In an era of newly emerging women professionals, in a culture where a college education began to be as common for a woman as for a man, in a country where the legal rights of women even in marriage were becoming a subject of debate, in a society coming awake to Simone de Beauvoir's *The Second Sex,* the image of the passive, invisible woman struck my generation as, if not passé, then at least suspect. Religious as well as secular feminists began to point out that classic conceptions of the role and person of Mary were at best really male images of women idealized. Where I myself was concerned, the figures of Teresa of Ávila, Catherine of Siena, and Joan of Arc—women who were adults in their own right, women who made a contribution to the spiritual life, women who got things done—meant more.

Clearly, devotion to Mary of Nazareth, the mother of Jesus, is not a subject that begins and ends with the liturgies, the prayers, or the traditions of the church. Devotion to Mary is not decided by theological formulations alone. When Carl Jung explored the relationship between psychology and religion, and with it the value of veneration for Mary to the human psyche, scholars of both religion and psychology raised their eyebrows in surprise, if not disbelief. What did devotion to Mary, an often discredited concept of Roman Catholicism, have to do either with psychology or with the role of faith in contemporary life? But Jung was not cautious in his conclusions. In fact, Jung may have understood the role of Marian devotion in Christian theology and human development in ways, perhaps, that other writers in the field did not.

Mary, Jung made clear, was not simply a woman shrouded in anonymity, lost to time and lacking in import. Jung wrote, "Mary was the instrument of God's birth and so became involved in the trinitarian drama as a human being. The Mother of God can, therefore, be regarded as a symbol of [hu]mankind's essential participation in the Trinity." She was, in other words, a bridge, an archetype, a sign, a symbol of the female energy in a God that had, despite the best theological definitions of the nature of God, become too male, too distant: too much judge, too little mother.

Jung uncovered what any serious review of the history of devotion to Mary would surely suggest: Mary was as important to the understanding of human development as she was to the theological constructs of the church; and, just as surely, she was as important to the theological constructs of the church as she was to any kind of personal piety or human maturation.

It is not surprising, then, that Mary has never been a nonfigure in Christianity. If anything, she has at some periods of history been more central to Christian sentiment than Jesus. What's more, she has always been as much a subject of theological discourse as she was a rendering of personal holiness.

Though biblical information on the person and life of Mary of Nazareth is sparse enough to be almost lacking, her very status as the mother of Jesus makes her a formidable theological personage. As such, she has ever raised important questions for the community of believers: What was the human and spiritual effect of this motherhood on her? On humankind in general? On the church? On the role and place and nature of women in particular?

Historical answers to those questions are wide ranging. In fact, vestiges of each are with us still. But not simply in theological tomes. Popular devotions express the *sensus fidelium,* the theological sense or understanding of the faithful, with regard to the place and person of Mary in Christian life. Some of these images of Mary have faded with time. Others persist no matter what official documents or scholarly interpretations say to contradict them. And it is in popular devotion that we see best the truth that while theology must inform devotion, that devotion must be informed by *popular* devotion, as well.

Two images of Mary emerge early in the history of the church. The first, embodied in the infancy narratives of Scripture, stresses the idea of her virginal conception of Jesus. The second, the notion of Mary's role as mediator, as suppliant, between the needs of people and the throne of God arises as early as the fourth or, some say, even the third century. Whether or not, as some scholars argue, this concept derives from the lingering strains of goddess worship transformed into Christian terms is interesting but not the only warrant for the idea. The fact is that the definition of Mary as "Mother of God" by the Council of Ephesus in 431 legitimated the question theologically. After all, if Jesus is both God and human as Ephesus proclaims, and Mary is the mother of Jesus, then Mary is also *Theotokos,* mother of God (literally, the "bearer of God"). Whether or not Mary has special intercessory power by virtue of her motherhood alone becomes, then, a constant question in the history of the church, right down to the time of Vatican II.

Patristic theologians—Irenaeus, Justin Martyr, Tertullian, and Ambrose, in particular—added another dimension to the nature of Marian devotion. Given to finding "types" in Scripture that spoke on the level of the metaphorical or symbolic as well as on the literal, they defined Mary as the "new Eve." Irenaeus's doctrine of *recirculatio,* the notion that evil is reversed in the same manner in which it came to be, made a convincing, and lasting, argument for Mary as prototype of the obedient woman. Eve, by this time the scapegoat for a sin that was Adam's as well as her own, pales in her sight. Mary, this theology postulates, by her obedience to the will of God "redeems" women—humankind—from the burden of degrading sinfulness. In the new Adam, Jesus—and the new Eve, Mary—the world begins again. Mary is clearly a "type" of Eve and a central figure in the Christian story, a commanding figure in the spiritual life.

Not surprisingly, then, by the Middle Ages, devotions based on Mary's intercessory power as miraculous Virgin, Mother of God, and New Eve—as instrument of salvation, God bearer, and sinless one—grew to exaggerated proportions. Mary came to be seen as the gentling hand of heaven in hard times. If God was remote from the people, if Latin liturgies distanced worshipers from the sacramental life of the church, if Scripture had no place in their lives, Mary nevertheless stayed accessible. Mary, they knew, was human, real, understanding—a mother. She was the compassionate one. God they saw in the midst of the plague as the harsh judge whose mind could be changed by her and her alone.

The Middle Ages became a Marian age. Other devotions dimmed in comparison. Songs, prayers, and litanies stressed her saving power, her intermediary influence, her heavenly centrality. It's in the Middle Ages that Marian antiphons are written that survive to this day. In this period, the Hail Mary becomes popular. And in this era, too, the Rosary begins to supplant the Divine Office, its Hail Marys substituting for the psalms. By this time, Mary is revered and appealed to at least as much as Jesus, if not more. But the counteraction was yet to come.

In the sixteenth century, Martin Luther and the Reformers also made Mary a central point in theology. But they questioned her centrality, her titles, the theological concepts—Mediator of All Graces, Queen of Heaven, Co-redeemer of Humankind—that were springing up in her behalf. Jesus Christ alone, they argued, ranks as mediator between God and humankind.

The point made for good theological disputation, perhaps, but bad reformation politics. Instead of restraining theological fervor for the role of the Mother of God in the heart of the faith, Mary became a defining point in Catholicism. By the seventeenth century, Protestant churches had all but eliminated any reference to Mariology whatsoever. For Catholics, on the other hand, devotion to Mary became a distinguishing feature of their tradition.

Whole religious congregations were dedicated to the name and honor of Mary. Commitment to her service became a mark of spirituality. Louis-Marie Grignon de Montfort (d. 1716) developed a Marian spirituality that required people to become "slaves of Mary." All favors were obtained by her from God, he argued; all actions were to be in her service. Now Mary had complete power over God. It was a devotion that reached all the way to my novitiate.

At first, I was secretly embarrassed to be so spiritually unaffected—even disconcerted—by the implications of such theology. As the years went by, however, I became more and more convinced that these concerns were not without merit, however much devotion to Mary marked the spirituality of the church itself. Nor was I alone in my dis-ease.

The Enlightenment era of the eighteenth century, with its emphasis on reason, dampened, at least for a while, the emotional excess that had crept into Marian devotion in Counter-Reformation times. Nineteenth-century romanticism, however, with its emphasis on feelings, introduced a new surge of both popular and ecclesiastical recognition that shaped twentieth-century devotion, as well. Apparition sites, the most famous of which were Lourdes, Guadalupe, Fatima, and, by the end of the century, Medugorje, became places of pilgrimage. Marian sodalities and May devotions became popular everywhere. The nine First Saturdays in honor of Mary ranked along with the nine First Fridays in privilege and indulgences. Mary—the passive, quiet, unquestioning Mary—became the Catholic girls' model of Catholic womanhood. And finally, the declaration of two Marian dogmas—her Immaculate Conception in 1854 and her Assumption into heaven in 1950—crowned centuries of Marian devotion with official recognition of her spiritual importance and stature.

And yet, something else had happened in the twentieth century. A new consciousness of the equality, full humanity, and social role of women swept the globe. Governments passed laws guaranteeing women civil rights, education, pay equity, legal protection, and equal participation in local, national, and international governing bodies. Women in the church became theologians, Scripture scholars, liturgists, and writers. Clearly, women had become anything but passive, quiet, and invisible.

With the changes in women themselves came the discovery of a Mary who had been anything but simply a pawn of the system. Theologians the rank of Karl Rahner, S.J., as well as a new generation of women scholars, began to see something very different in the story of Mary than what had been defined before them.

New litanies in her name spoke of her strength of mind, her willingness to confront systems, her prophetic witness to the life and work of Jesus, as well as her presence at Pentecost—with everything that implied. Women—I myself—began to see Mary emerge in Scripture as someone called by God to save the people, as Moses and Abraham had ever been. This Mary, I began to realize, was independent and strong. She was a woman who knew exile. She had braved social rejection for the sake of the will of

God. She knew suffering and poverty and powerlessness, just as women everywhere did. But she was a woman who never gave in to institutional restrictions and never gave up her right to shape her world. This was a woman who never doubted the word of God for her, whatever the system said to the contrary. She had debated with angels. She had asked no male, neither Joseph nor the high priests, for permission to do what she knew God was calling her to do. Through her, the will of God was turned into the body and blood of Jesus. Through her visit to Elizabeth, she supported other women in their own call. Through her faith, faith grew. She directed the ministry of Jesus at the wedding feast of Cana. She sang Magnificat of liberation. She believed all the way to the cross and then went on beyond it.

All of a sudden, it became very clear: Mary was the feminine energy in Christianity. That's why every age was drawn to her. That's why no age has abandoned her. That's why both men and women find the missing piece of Christianity in her.

Indeed theological concerns still abound: How much devotion to Mary is too much devotion? Which elements of the image and ministry of Mary are still missing in Christianity? What is her rightful, her determining place in Christian life and spirituality? The struggle to define goes on to this day. The movement to grant Mary the titles of "Coredemptrix" and "Mediatrix of All Graces" gained new impetus under the papacy of John Paul II, despite the decision of the council fathers of Vatican II to table such a motion.

But history is clear: it doesn't much matter what kind of official definitions of Mary obtain. In the end, it's the *sensus fidelium,* the awareness in the hearts of the faithful that Mary is at the heart of the tradition, that, as it has in the past, will certainly prevail.

The Liturgy
of the Hours

ELIZABETH COLLIER, thirty-two, is the director of the Crossroads Center for Faith and Work, in Chicago. A native of Peoria, Iowa, she is a graduate of Creighton University in Omaha, and in 1998 she received her master's degree in divinity at Weston Jesuit School of Theology in Cambridge, Massachusetts. Today Ms. Collier is completing her Ph.D. dissertation on Christian social ethics at Loyola University Chicago, where she teaches an undergraduate course on urban poverty. She lives with her husband, Jeremy Langford, and their newborn son, Tyler, in Evanston, Illinois.

....

Having spent the past fifteen years at various Jesuit institutions, I have probably logged more hours on retreats, in spiritual direction, in prayer groups, discussing or teaching theological topics, and doing or organizing service work than your average thirtysomething. But despite all of the above, I am embarrassed to say that for the past few years I have not spent much time praying, and when I have, it has not been as fruitful as I would like. This is due, in large part, to the pace of my life. As with many people I know, I am overcommitted and juggle too much responsibility. Each night, I collapse, very much aware of all I was unable to accomplish during the day.

To fill the void of my poor prayer life, I've often browsed through the many meditation books and resources for "busy people." Yet nothing I have tried has yielded more than just a feeling of fulfilling an obligation. My search was for something with the depth and beauty that so many other aspects of our faith offer. But how to find a middle ground among my spiritual desires, the scriptural call to "pray ceaselessly," and the constraints on my time and energy?

Last spring the U.S. Cistercian novice directors asked my husband and me to meet with them in

Snowmass, Colorado, to help them better understand Generation X. Having had no experience with a cloistered religious community, I arrived at the meeting somewhat skeptical, even suspicious, of their vocation. The Jesuit charism surrounding social justice and phrases like "contemplatives in action" were what encapsulated my ideals of Christian service. I didn't really understand how a cloistered life could be a "ministry" to the church or the world, or how monastic men and women were "bringing about the kingdom of God." But after several days of meetings, meals, and late-night conversations, I came to admire the Cistercian life and saw far more connections between our two vocations than I would have imagined. These were healthy, interesting, intelligent, and deeply spiritual people, whose time living in a community of work and prayer had given them insights into their own talents as well as the challenges they faced within their communities.

Cistercian time is punctuated by praying the Liturgy of the Hours and by practicing mindfulness during the day's work. And although I am not called to their particular vocation, I longed for a way of marking my own days with similar rhythms of prayer.

After returning to Chicago, I committed myself to more regular prayer. In my home library I found a two-volume set of books that I had bought several years before but had never used: a layperson's guide to the Liturgy of the Hours. I decided to take up the texts on my own terms, adapting them to my vocation and lifestyle without learning the rubrics or even much of the history. I didn't want to get caught up in too many "should's" but wanted instead to explore how God might be able to break into my contemporary life through this ancient tradition. As it has for centuries, morning and evening prayer includes several psalms, a brief reading from a saint, theologian, or spiritual writer, a responsorial psalm, the canticle of Zechariah or of Mary, prayer petitions, and a short prayer to begin or end the day.

After spending time with these prayers and, later, learning about the history of the Liturgy of the Hours, I found many aspects of the practice particularly suited to what I had been seeking. With its roots in ancient Jewish rituals, its later adaptation by the early Christian community, and its continued daily use throughout Christian history, I also felt a profound historical connection with the countless generations who punctuated their days in similar ways. Especially valuable for me is the prayer experience offered by the version I use. It combines ancient psalms and canticles, readings from the church fathers, medieval saints, and modern women, along with intercessions that relate to the challenges of contemporary socioeconomic structures and environmental concerns.

The historical development of the devotion also exemplified the adaptability and flexibility I had been searching for. From as early as the fourth and fifth centuries, attempts by Christians to integrate regular prayer times into their busy lives resulted in the flowering of two different traditions for praying the Liturgy of the Hours. The "monastic" tradition reflected the fact that life in a monastery allowed for a more frequent and time-intensive focus on the psalms and prayer periods throughout the day and night. In turn, what came to be known as the "cathedral" tradition developed for the laity; this tradition called people to pray as a community in the morning and evening, and included shorter meditations and fewer psalms. The cathedral tradition accommodated the workaday life of the average person.

But from the twelfth century on, outside of monasteries the practice became primarily a private, clerical devotion. The laity began to focus increasingly on shorter prayers and devotions like the Rosary, which could be done either privately or within a church community. (The Rosary itself, with its original fifteen "decades" of prayers, was a deliberate abbreviation of the 150 psalms.) Today, priests and deacons are still required to pray the Liturgy of the Hours daily, and the Second Vatican Council called for the devotion to be incorporated more into parish life. The council's "Constitution on the Sacred Liturgy" asked pastors to see that at least some portion of the Liturgy of the Hours was observed in their parishes—for example, at a service of Sunday vespers.

In addition to the historical tradition of the devotion, it touches me deeply to think that people throughout the world, from all walks of life, are praying with similar texts each day. It provides an almost tangible connectedness that inspires me in the solitude of my home office. When I am able to pray in the morning, it brings a mindfulness to the gift of the day, which often stays with me after I walk out the door. The text itself provides not only the comforting repetition found in the Mass, but also enough variety that I have less of a tendency to "go through the motions," as I do with other forms of prayer. By following the liturgical year I feel connected to the seasons of the church year in a way that I enjoyed when daily Mass was still an option for my schedule. And the readings for feast days offer me insights into the lives of inspiring men and women. Overall, the various prayers and readings touch upon the struggles and celebrations that occur in all of our lives.

Admittedly, I do not pray the Liturgy of the Hours as diligently as I might, nor do I replicate the total commitment of the monastic communities.

But the connection I feel to a larger praying community helps with this. If I can pray only once a day or miss prayer altogether, I know that thousands of others are carrying on this living tradition for the good of all creation. If I begin praying the office and discover an image or phrase that attracts my attention, my Ignatian education kicks in, and I realize that God may be drawing me toward a more specific word or phrase to focus on. And on days when I actually pray the morning, afternoon, and evening hours, I know that I have taken up the call to prayer for those who were unable to pray.

It is ironic that a trip intended to offer a cloistered community insight into a generation that grew up in the midst of constant activity would result in my incorporating an ancient contemplative practice into an action-oriented Christian life. It seems a special testament to the Spirit, who brings forth elements of our tradition that have been life-giving for previous generations in ways that are fruitful and adaptable in the midst of contemporary challenges.

Novenas

DIANNE BERGANT, C.S.A., a member of the Congregation of St. Agnes, is professor of biblical studies at Catholic Theological Union in Chicago, Illinois. An active member of the Chicago Catholic-Jewish Scholars Dialogue for the past seventeen years, she also serves on the editorial boards of *The Bible Today* and *Biblical Theological Bulletin*. Sister Dianne is the author of a number of books, including *Song of Songs: The Love Poetry of Scripture, Preaching the Lectionary,* and *People of the Covenant: An Invitation to the Old Testament*. She also writes "The Word" column for *America* magazine, a weekly reflection on Scripture.

....

I grew up three blocks from St. Mary, Help of Christians Church in West Allis, Wisconsin. At the time, the parish sponsored no school, so my sister and I were enrolled in the school of a neighboring parish. But with the exception of school events, my entire religious life centered around St. Mary's. I went to Mass there, sang in the choir, and every Tuesday attended the novena in honor of the Mother of Perpetual Help. To this day I remember the hymns and many of the prayers. This particular novena was not like other novenas, which consist of some successive pattern of nine days: it was an ongoing weekly parish devotion. In a sense, the novena itself was perpetual.

While I doubt that as a child I understood the religious implications of the novena, I always felt that it was important to attend. I don't recall ever having a pressing need to bring to the attention of the Mother of God, and it wasn't until I was an adult that I discovered that this particular devotion was part of the ethnic culture of the parish. Still, the Perpetual Help novena was as much a part of the religious landscape of my young life as were altar bells, incense, and Easter lilies. They offered me a sense of belonging to a religious world and, in turn, a sense of belonging to God.

Novenas have a long history. The typical period of mourning that the ancient Greeks and Romans observed extended through nine days and culminated with a feast. The pagan character of the practice so offended Christians that they shortened their mourning period to seven days in order to distinguish themselves from nonbelievers. Sometime during the Middle Ages, Christmas novenas, which called to mind the nine months of Mary's pregnancy, began to appear in France and Spain. (The liturgical use of the "O Antiphons" in the days before Christmas is a remnant of this practice.) Other liturgical novenas arose, most notably one that precedes the Feast of Pentecost. This is based on the biblical account of the disciples, who, after the ascension of the Lord, waited nine days for the coming of the Spirit (Lk 24:49; Acts 1:4).

The novena is sometimes confused with the octave. The latter is an eight-day extension of the celebration of a feast, for example, the octave of

Christmas. A novena, on the other hand, usually consists of a nine-day period of intercession prompted by some urgent need. Whereas an octave follows the event that commemorates a manifestation of God's goodness, a novena asks that God's goodness be granted. An octave is joyful; a novena is marked by a degree of urgent anticipation. At least this was originally the case.

In the seventeenth century the character of the novena began to change. While remaining a form of petitionary prayer, it also became a way of honoring the one to whom the novena was directed. Around this time novenas in honor of Mary, under any number of titles, sprang up across Europe. Some religious communities also began to pray novenas in honor of their major patrons. Others developed the practice of preparing for major liturgical feasts by means of a novena. In the nineteenth century the church began granting indulgences for the faithful performance of certain novenas. The *Raccolta,* the official book of indulgences, lists more than thirty indulgenced novenas.

Today novenas play a role in my own life not unlike the role they played when I was a child. In other words, the novena is more a part of my religious culture than of my personal devotion. This is not to imply that it has lost its importance; rather, to repeat the image used above, it is part of the religious landscape of my life—now as a member of my religious community. Like most communities, we Sisters of St. Agnes commemorate our patronal feasts with preparatory prayer, and in many of our houses this continues to assume the form of a novena. As part of our religious heritage, such common celebrations have created among us a communal identity and have strengthened the bonds that unite us.

Novenas may have originated during the Middle Ages, but they are certainly not outdated devotions. St. Agnes, for example, has traditionally been considered a patron of chastity. But her refusal to respond to an officially arranged marriage was, at that time in history, primarily a courageous act against the state. Today we Sisters of St. Agnes pray for the courage to stand firm in our religious convictions regardless of the political consequences. Another patronal feast we celebrate is the Immaculate Conception, the Marian title under which the United States was dedicated to the Blessed Mother. Our novena in preparation for that feast often centers on the pressing religious needs of our country. In such ways, community novenas provide us with periods of time to consider ways of remaining faithful to our religious commitment within the context of the contemporary world.

For me, the celebrations of these patronal feasts have recently taken on a totally new relevance and importance. Understanding the depth and power of the patrons' commitment and interpreting anew the religious issues with which they are associated have made their witness a real challenge. And the novenas in their honor provide me with time to reflect on the significance of these issues for my own life. Such novenas enable me to celebrate the respective feast in the religious spirit of the patron and not merely with a festive meal. Perhaps most significant, novenas have become times of preparation for some change that I must make in my life rather than times of "storming heaven" for a favor.

It's not surprising that religious communities with roots in centuries past continue the practice of novenas. But what about modern-day Christians—those who have little time and less patience for periods of preparation, those who expect things to happen with the flick of a switch or the tap of a computer key? Would they find any value in a novena?

Why not? Most people today are in fact well acquainted with long periods of preparation. If anything, the complexity of modern life shows that adequate preparation—think of how many years of education are needed in some professions—is essential for success in life. On another, more intimate level, the nine months of pregnancy allow time for everyone involved to prepare not only for the anticipated birth itself but also for the unfolding of life after the child is born. In general, then, I don't think one can argue that people no longer have the patience to "wait."

Some may also argue that novenas fail to capture the contemporary religious imagination because they do not encourage individuals to involve themselves in any pressing contemporary needs. And if anything, the events of September 11, 2001, showed that modern-day people do indeed respond to urgent need. The tragedy touched a chord in the hearts of millions who, in response, thronged the streets and filled places of worship. Novenas, as I have discovered in my own life, can be a wonderful way to consider and reflect on such pressing and urgent needs. Perhaps, then, it is time to look again at the ancient practice of novenas, which engage us in the joy of expectation and the holiness of commitment, as a way of directing such powerful religious sentiments.

Our Lady of Guadalupe

ERIC STOLTZ, forty-three, is a native Angeleno who attended Catholic elementary and high schools. After spending twenty years as a public-relations executive, he became a self-taught Web developer specializing in sites for not-for-profit organizations, eventually creating an online Catholic journal, *hosea.org*. A frequent contributor to *America* and other national Catholic publications, he is a candidate for ordination to the diaconate for the Archdiocese of Los Angeles.

....

Here in *El Pueblo de Nuestra Señora la Reina de los Ángeles,* "The City of Our Lady, Queen of the Angels," a city most people know as Los Angeles, one cannot go long without encountering Our Lady of Guadalupe. She gazes tranquilly from the stucco walls of convenience stores, from the black dashboards of cars, from gold medallions, from the blue ink of tattoos.

Her story and my people's traditions surrounding *la Virgen* remain powerful because she speaks to the deepest recesses of the human soul. For more than four hundred years before the Second Vatican Council's "Pastoral Constitution on the Church in the Modern World" (1965), she was teaching an entire people every day how to share the joy and hope, the grief and anxiety of the whole human race.

There was snow on the ground that December morning of 1531 when a poor fifty-seven-year-old Aztec widower named Juan Diego Cuauhtlatzin approached Tepeyac Hill on his fifteen-mile walk to Mass. He climbed the hill because he heard music and someone softly calling his name: *¡Juanito! ¡Juan Dieguito!* It was an affectionate form of his name, as though she were calling, "Johnny! Little John Diego!" There he encountered a young Indian woman, dark like him, wearing traditional Aztec garb, including the black sash around her waist indicating she was pregnant.

She told him she was Mary and that she desired a church to be built there, where she could hear her people's weeping and sorrows and console them. He was to inform the bishop of Mexico City of her request. Bishop Zumárraga was a proud Spaniard, and he shooed away this ignorant Indian. Juan Diego reported the bishop's dismissal to the lady. She sent him back. The bishop again sent him away disdainfully, this time demanding a miracle.

His Excellency got his miracle and then some. When Juan Diego arrived at the bishop's palace the third time, he dumped out roses the lady had picked from Tepeyac's snowy rocks and arranged in his rough cloak, his *tilma*. There on his cloak was the image of the very lady he had met on the hill, an image preserved to this day in the basilica dedicated to her outside Mexico City.

On Tepeyac Mary did not threaten calamity, or tell the pope to say a certain prayer on a particular day, or confirm a fine point of Augustinian theology.

She promised only to listen to anyone who would come to her. She offered only companionship, compassion, and consolation. But this simple gift has resonated through the world for hundreds of years, an earthy song of divine pathos sung by millions of voices that only grows stronger with time.

The second gift we experience at Tepeyac is that she comes to us as we are and speaks our language. Zumárraga could not believe that Mary would speak the "pagan" Nahuatl language of Juan Diego. When he told the bishop the lady called herself *Tequantlaxopeuh* ("she who crushes the serpent's head"), the Spaniard assumed he meant *"de Guadalupe,"* referring to a shrine in Spain. At that time Bartolomé de Las Casas was still debating the theologians of Europe's most prestigious universities to prove indigenous people were human beings, so perhaps we should not be surprised that Zumárraga would assume Mary was European. We all hear what we expect to hear, but sometimes God's word is entirely unexpected and its messenger even more unlikely.

The third gift of Tepeyac deals with issues of authority. In the story, the bishop is the obstacle, and the conquered peasant carries the world-changing message. This is why, in my world, when her oppressed children cry out—whether janitors massing at city hall, or farm workers protesting along a dusty road in California's Central Valley, or gay and lesbian Catholics marching down Santa Monica Boulevard, *anawim* of every stripe—they always carry an image of Our Lady of Guadalupe. We know she walks with us. Impoverished, immigrant, indigenous, or "intrinsically disordered," we remember her words of assurance to Juan Diego: *¿No soy tu madre?* ("Am I not your mother?") Yes, we remember. We remember with a memory of centuries that can only be described as pondering these things in our hearts.

If I wish to clothe myself in the reality of the Magnificat, I cut my own life's pattern tracing the story of Tepeyac. If I am denied a job because of who I am, if I am denounced in the halls of Congress as a godless outsider, derided as a pragmatically deprived idealist, as a troublemaker, as someone who asks the question everyone else is afraid to ask, as someone whose refusal to play by the rules makes others think I just don't get it, or just as someone scorned on the street, then the story of Tepeyac comes alive in me. The story reminds me that my Father and my Mother accept and love me for all the reasons that move others to despise me. When powers are arrayed against me, when the proud look down from their thrones, I am Juan Diego; I open my *tilma* and flowers cascade from it. I revel in my weakness. And I am lifted up.

On Tepeyac stands a lady who shelters the oppressed, the marginalized, those who are less-than. She trusts me to carry a message without having a fancy title. She hears me in my despair and comforts me. But she also teaches me the power of love, love despite all tribulation, a screaming, starving love fed only with hope.

Relics

MELANIE McDONAGH, an Irish journalist who lives in Britain, is a contributing writer to the *Tablet*. Her doctoral research at the University of Cambridge was on the subject of medieval devotion to St. John the Baptist.

....

In the cathedral church of Amiens, in Picardy, there is a relic of quite remarkable distinction. It is the head of St. John the Baptist. Or if we are to be precise, the frontal part of the skull. There, set into the wall, is the sacred head that was separated from its body at the behest of a dancing girl, and on the remarkable painted sixteenth-century choir screen opposite, the whole melancholy story is depicted of the life and death of St. John.

What is interesting about the relic, from my point of view, is that all by itself it added a new and piquant episode to the Gospel account of John's decapitation. On the skull there is a puncture mark above the eye. And when the relic was brought to Amiens at the beginning of the thirteenth century, there was only one possible construction that could be placed on this circumstance. On the choir screen depiction of Herod's banquet, we can see what it was. As the head is presented to Herodias on a platter, the adulteress brings down her carving knife onto it, causing the head to be punctured—and thus accounting for the hole. Thus, the relic spoke: it related the story of the decapitation of the Baptist mutely. From Amiens, the legend spread, into art and the saint plays on the Baptist.

That's the nice thing about relics: they have a life of their own. To regard relics merely as passive, quiescent, and rather horrid bits of the dead that in more tasteful times would be safely buried is to miss the point of them. In the days when they were held in highest esteem—from the fifth to the sixteenth centuries—relics were never merely mementos of the holy dead. They gave, in themselves, a kind of continuity with the life of the saint; the vicissitudes of his body mimicked its tribulations in life; and the merits worked by the relics bore testimony to his sanctity. What is more, the relationship between devotees of a saint and his relics—which might, of course, be objects associated with him as well as parts of his body—had a peculiar kind of dynamic.

To explain, let me stick with the relic of St. John. It arrived in Amiens in 1206, borne in great state by its donor, a canon of the cathedral called Wallo, or Walon. The means whereby Wallo had acquired this extraordinary gift was perfectly simple. He had been in Constantinople during the Crusades and had stolen the head from the Church of St. George by dint of hiding in the church after evening prayers were over and passing the head through the church window to a female accomplice outside. It was, of course, theft, and it was moreover theft at the expense of the unfortunate monks of the church, who had much prized their head. It was, in short, a classic instance of *furtum sacrum,* or holy theft. The gist of the theory behind the phenomenon was that the theft of relics indicated proper devotion to the saint concerned, and also demonstrated that the relics were not—evidently—in safe hands in the first place. More than that, it was plainly the will of the saint that his body part should be removed to a more worthy location, because otherwise he would not have allowed the theft to happen.

All this is meant in no abstract fashion. The interesting feature of the behavior of the bodies of the saints in medieval legend is that they were not merely commodities to be passed from hand to hand. They had, if you like, a will of their own. A characteristic feature of any number of hagiographies is that the saint himself expressed himself through his body, in that, when it was being carried by devotees from its original place of repose, it would indicate where it wished to rest. And it usually did so by becoming impossibly heavy to carry further when it had reached its desired home. The reciprocity of the relationship between relics and their devotees is even more vividly recalled in the fact that when relics did not work and failed to provide the protection that they should for the place where they reposed, the slight did not go unpunished. There is an extraordinary medieval rite for the humiliation, or degradation, of relics, whereby an underperforming relic would be systematically dishonored in order to recall the saint to a sense of his obligations.

Nowadays our view of the dead is extraordinarily sanitized, at least in the West. The notion of exhibiting body parts or corpses in imperfect states of decomposition, even in gold settings, has an undoubtedly gross aspect for the sensitive viewer. But the truth is that the early church had quite a different attitude toward the sacred dead. Many early Christian communities grew up around the tombs of the martyrs, where the faithful could share in the radiant merits of the tortured bodies, which bore witness to their sufferings on earth.

The drawback to this proximity to the sacred was that it was limited to those people fortunate enough to have access to their tombs. For the merits of the saints to be more widely shared, it was necessary for their bodies to be broken and fractured, and disseminated to those Christian communities living remote from the martyrs' tombs. And this is precisely what relics did. They were a means of reinforcing the Christian community, by sharing the merits of a saint with far-flung groups of Christians. Bede's *Ecclesiastical History of the English People,* for instance, is enlivened by accounts of bishops going to Rome or receiving from Rome relics of the apostles and saints, which grounded the young Anglo-Saxon church in the wider apostolic church. This was no abstract communion, but reinforced in a concrete, fleshly fashion. That is what relics do: they unite the present with the past, the contemporary Christian community with the church of the saints.

By the late Middle Ages, the devotion attached to the saints' bodies had shifted to devotion to images of the saints, which were more easily and widely disseminated. And that tradition is still with us. In

Amiens, the head of John the Baptist—admittedly one of the three heads of which I know—stands solitary. A little distance away, the statue of, I think, St. Anthony has dozens of candles before it. Plainly, we have missed the point of relics. They are an opportunity to experience proximity to the saints, their sheer carnality, their sameness with us and their difference from us. Catholicism revolves around things that we can touch and see, and relics are a preeminent example of this unabashed physicality of the faith. Relics unite the present with the past. Those dry bones speak.

Adoration of the Blessed Sacrament

BRIAN E. DALEY, S.J., a Jesuit priest, is the Catherine F. Huisking Professor of Theology at the University of Notre Dame and a specialist in early Christian theology. A graduate of the University of Oxford, he has also taught at the Weston Jesuit School of Theology in Cambridge, Massachusetts. Fr. Daley is Catholic executive secretary of the North American Orthodox-Catholic Consultation and past president of the North American Patristic Society. His most recent book is *The Hope of the Early Church: A Handbook of Patristic Eschatology.*

....

In the current practice of the Catholic Church in the United States, people are free to receive communion either in the open hand or on the tongue.

Although I have not conducted a survey, my impression from presiding at both student and parish liturgies is that the practice tends to vary largely along lines of age: most of the people to whom I give communion on the tongue, at least here at Notre Dame, seem to be under thirty-five. And while I have never attempted to find out why so many young Catholics seem to prefer this practice, I suspect it is part of a more general desire on the part of their generation to find physical, not merely verbal, ways of expressing and deepening a reverent awareness of the mystery of Christ's presence in the Eucharist.

The subject of how best to express reverence for what we Catholics so dryly call the eucharistic "species" has become a contentious one in the church. It touches on church architecture and inner arrangement—for instance where to place the tabernacle in which the Host is reserved and how to coordinate the placement of the tabernacle with the lectern where Scripture is read. It also includes a variety of traditional practices some would like to revive among the faithful: keeping a reverent silence in church, even outside times of liturgical celebration; genuflecting when passing in front of the tabernacle; making a profound bow before receiving communion. Many who promote these practices feel that the liturgical changes instituted since the Second Vatican Council have unintentionally communicated to Catholics a secular spirit, in which the church building has become more a meeting place, a place for human conversation, than a sacred place where the transcendent God encounters us in human gestures and things.

One Catholic practice on which these changing sensibilities have been focused is eucharistic adoration, a period of quiet prayer in a space primarily intended for liturgical worship—prayer focused on the sacramental bread, either reserved in a locked tabernacle or exposed to view in a monstrance. When I was growing up, this kind of devotion to the Eucharist outside the Mass was central to my developing faith, my sense of the real possibility of finding God in the life of a New Jersey parish. When Catholics in the 1950s or 1960s passed a church, it was common practice to stop in for a brief "visit" to the Lord present in the Blessed Sacrament. In that quiet place, the darkness punctuated only by a few flickering vigil lights, one had a sense that God was suddenly close, a hidden spring of life just under the surface of daily routine. Benediction of the Blessed Sacrament, a fifteen-minute service involving the exposition of the eucharistic bread, a few familiar Latin hymns, prayers, incense, and a multitude of candles, was the normal conclusion to services other than the Mass—to novenas, vespers, and the programmatic preaching of the Catholic equivalent of a revival: the parish mission. Likewise, Holy Thursday included not only a solemn liturgy and procession, commemorating the institution of the Eucharist at Jesus' Last Supper, but also long periods of silent prayer afterward before the sacrament itself, now moved from its normal place in the tabernacle to an altar of "repose" in some other part of the church.

Once a year, each parish celebrated the Forty Hours Devotion, too, in honor of the Blessed Sacrament—a kind of three-day community marathon of silent prayer before the exposed host, now raised high over the altar and surrounded with banks of flowers and shimmering candles. For me as a child and a teenager, these forms of eucharistic devotion were an introduction to a peculiarly Catholic form of contemplative prayer: a prayer not so much of withdrawal from things of the senses as of kneeling and gazing, of awestruck adoration in the midst of a throng of other worshipers. With a bit of imagination, one easily felt the words of the hymn had become real: as "all mortal flesh kept silence," the "heavenly vanguard" of angels and saints joined us in this act of ecclesial reverence. It was something richly sensual, yet pointing—through the focal point of a small white wafer—to the fullness of the church, to the heavenly liturgy, and to Jesus the eternal priest.

As in so many other aspects of Catholic life, eucharistic devotion of this sort largely disappeared from the church's normal agenda in the late 1960s. The Eucharist, it was often pointed out, is a ritual meal, in which the whole community, gathered under the representative headship of a bishop or a priest, worships God as one body and is nourished by the word of Scripture and the signs of Jesus' sacrifice. The purpose of the eucharistic species, then, is not to be the object of adoration but the daily food of God's "pilgrim people." The Second Vatican Council's "Constitution on the Sacred Liturgy" states that "devotions" practiced in the church, important as they are, must be "controlled so that they cohere with the sacred liturgy, in some way derive from it, and lead the people to it" (no. 13). It also emphasizes the central importance of Scripture and the homily in the Mass (no. 24), and stresses that liturgy is by its nature not a time for private prayer, but the community's public celebration (nos. 26–28). In a famous passage, the same document explicitly broadens the notion of Christ's "presence" in liturgical celebration to include not only his presence in the eucharistic species (where he is found "most fully"—*maxime*) but also in the other sacraments, in the person of the presider, in the word of Scripture, and in the whole congregation gathered in Christ's name (no. 7).

All of this doubtless came as a needed correction of post-Reformation imbalances in the Catholic Church's life of worship. Yet it has led to some new imbalances as well: to a new emphasis on words in Catholic worship, with a corresponding de-emphasis of concrete, time-hallowed symbols; to a rationalistic barrenness in some modern church architecture and decoration; to an emphasis on community formation rather than adoration of God as the implied goal of some Sunday assemblies; to a bland moralism in a good deal of contemporary Catholic preaching and an occasional tendency to self-celebration in contemporary liturgical music. So a new reaction has been under way since at least the early 1990s, as the young seek to find contact again with the church's symbolic world and with the divine, living presence it embodies, while their elders seek to discern between healthy impulse and baroque excess in the devotional life of the church of their youth.

In this context, eucharistic adoration seems to be exerting a renewed attraction on young Catholics who seek to draw wisdom from the riches of the church's tradition. Renewed official guidelines for this devotion now offer a variety of forms that services of eucharistic adoration might take, incorporating readings, a homily, and a variety of prayers, as well as quiet contemplation, hymns, and the climactic blessing of the congregation with the eucharistic body of Christ.[1] If used with imagination, these guidelines promise a way of reviving eucharistic adoration within the framework of the liturgical year and the liturgical day: not as a substitute for the Mass, but as an occasion to let the heart of the Mass—our encounter with the risen Jesus in the sacramental signs of bread and wine, and in the sacramental narrative of God's saving history—become the continuing object of our thought and gaze, and invite us to deeper, more conscious participation in the eucharistic meal.

This devotional instinct has deep roots in the Western, Catholic tradition of Christianity. Since the thirteenth century, I would suggest, the eucharistic "species," and particularly the eucharistic bread, has played a role in the church's devotional life similar to that of icons in the Orthodox tradition: both have been seen, not just by theologians but by all the faithful, as more than simply external representations of holy people and holy acts. Rather, they are seen as windows between our sensible world and the heavenly realm, as manifestations in visible form of God's transcendent glory, nourishing and transforming our humanity, reaching us where we are. In the Orthodox churches, the first Sunday of Great Lent is called the "Sunday of Orthodoxy," precisely because on that day Orthodox Christians commemorate the official restoration of the veneration of icons in 843, after more than a century of bitter conflict about the legitimacy of their use in devotional practice. Just as the icon expresses for Orthodox believers the heart of their Christian identity—their sense of how God is with us in human beings—the eucharistic bread is, for Catholics, not only the "body of Christ" in the sacramental sense, but the quintessential icon of the larger Body of Christ, which is the church. To pray in wonder before this sign still seems to me a central, even indispensable, part of sharing the life of that Body.

Praying before the Sacred Host continues to play an important part in my own life. Although the opportunities for formal eucharistic adoration are fewer now than when I was young, I still find the practice moving and nurturing, understated yet strangely grand. I find, too, that my routine of morning prayer, carried out in our small Jesuit community chapel in the presence of the Blessed Sacrament in the tabernacle, seems decidedly more focused, more personal, more consoling than prayer in my own room. Prayer before the Eucharist also has an inescapable churchly dimension that other forms of private prayer may lack. This is the sign, after all, around which the church gathers, to discover and nourish its authentic self as the collective Body of Christ. As St. Augustine remarks in an Easter homily, "If you are the Body and the members of Christ, your own Mystery is placed on the table of the Lord—you receive your own Mystery" (Sermon 272). The attraction of eucharistic devotion, for me at least, is that it enables us to spend time simply trying to encounter that multifaceted Body as something immediate and visibly real. Prayer is always an encounter with Mystery, but it seems more obvious to me, as I pray before the Blessed Sacrament, that the Lord is *there,* and that in the stillness of a little room I am somehow at the heart of the church.

Acknowledgments

First, I would like to thank all of the writers who so generously contributed to this collection. Their willingness to reveal some of their own faith, as well as the time they spent in preparing (and researching) their essays, is, needless to say, greatly appreciated. Thanks also to Kevin White, S.J., one of the essayists, who pointed me to the Vatican document on the devotional life. I am grateful to Janice Farnham, R.J.M., another contributor, who helped me understand more precisely what a devotion *is*. And thanks to Kevin O'Brien, S.J., and Dave Nantais, S.J., for helping me brainstorm about the title.

Most of these essays originally appeared as part of a Lenten and Easter series in *America* magazine, so I want to thank Robert Collins, S.J., managing editor, for his help in the complicated (at least to me) task of translating the computer files. Thanks also to Thomas Reese, S.J., the magazine's editor in chief, for his encouragement in my work on the original series and on this book as well. Shaila Dani, an intern at *America,* helped enormously with the editing and the typing of the final manuscript. As for this book, and as the saying goes, I couldn't have done it without her. I am most grateful.

At Loyola Press, George Lane, S.J., Jim Manney, Matthew Diener, and Mark Colucci were wonderfully efficient and cheerful as they helped to guide this book to completion.

Finally, since my first devotion (though I wouldn't have known to call it that) was to the Rosary, I thank my mother and father, who gave me that particular gift on the day of my first Holy Communion, over thirty years ago.

Notes

INTRODUCTION

1. "Constitution on the Sacred Liturgy," no. 13, in *The Documents of Vatican II,* ed. Walter M. Abbott, S.J. (New York: America Press, 1966), 143.

2. Congregation for Divine Worship and the Discipline of the Sacraments, "Directory on Popular Piety and the Liturgy: Principles and Guidelines" (Vatican City: 2001), no. 58.

3. Ibid., no. 1.

4. Regis A. Duffy, "Devotions," in *The Encyclopedia of Catholicism,* ed. Richard McBrien (New York: HarperCollins, 1995), 414.

5. Carl Dehne, S.J., "Devotions," in *The New Dictionary of Theology,* ed. Joseph A. Komonchak, Mary Collins, and Dermot A. Lane (Collegeville, Minn.: Liturgical Press, 1987), 283–88.

6. Congregation for Divine Worship and the Discipline of the Sacraments, "Directory," nos. 7–10.

Notes

THE ROSARY

1. St. Thérèse of Lisieux, *Story of a Soul,* trans. John Clarke, O.C.D. (Washington, D.C.: ICS Publications, 1976), 242–43.

PILGRIMAGE

1. International Commission on English in the Liturgy, National Conference of Catholic Bishops, *The Roman Ritual: Book of Blessings* (New York: Catholic Book Publishing, 1989), 260.

2. Ibid., 263.

ADORATION OF THE BLESSED SACRAMENT

1. See National Conference of Catholic Bishops, *Eucharistic Worship and Devotion outside Mass* (Washington, D.C.: Office for Publishing and Promotion Services, U.S. Catholic Conference, 1987).

About the Editor

JAMES MARTIN, S.J., is a Jesuit priest and associate editor of *America,* a national Catholic magazine. A graduate of the Wharton School of Business, he worked for six years in corporate finance before entering the Society of Jesus in 1988. During his Jesuit training he worked at a hospice for the sick and dying in Kingston, Jamaica, with street-gang members in Chicago, as a prison chaplain in Boston, and for two years with East African refugees in Nairobi, Kenya. After completing his theological studies he was ordained a priest in 1999. Fr. Martin's writing has appeared in a variety of newspapers and magazines, and he is the author of a number of books, including *In Good Company: The Fast Track from the Corporate World to Poverty, Chastity, and*

Obedience (Sheed & Ward, 2000) and *This Our Exile: A Spiritual Journey with the Refugees of East Africa* (Orbis, 1999).